DOUBLEDIPITY:
MORE SERENDIPITY QUILTS

BY SARA NEPHEW

Tattler (facing page back) 83" x 98¼", is an old-fashioned looking quilt thanks to the 2-Row TAT-TLER block. Lots of fabric found at a garage sale means lots of blocks, and the more blocks you make the more fun you have with stacked repeats. The author mixed background fabrics and finished corners with half-blocks.

Starburst (facing page right) 58" x 89½".
The soft suede-look browns in this quilt top give the design a Native American look. There's a lot going on here! Marylou devised a new elongated layout, finished at the corners with stacked hexes in diamonds. Then the leftover stripped triangles combine in interesting border panels. Finally, notice the miniature blocks featured in the borders. Lots of creative originality!
Pieced by Marylou Sommer.

Hot Tamale (facing page left) 53" x 58¼".
Grey stripes combine with red, yellow, and orange to look like fire, coals, and ashes. Everything is burning!
The stripped triangles in the border are placed to make small hexagons in diamonds - another border inspiration. A primitive look with lots of design strength.
Pieced by Diane Coombs.

OUTLINE

DOUBLEDIPITY:
MORE SERENDIPITY QUILTS

SPECIAL THANKS

To the pattern testers, who enjoy setting their stamp of color, texture, and design onto a black and white untried pattern. I owe them for new layouts, new borders, new points of view. They are good designers. This time sincere thanks are due to: Virginia Anderson, Bonnie Chambers, Diane Coombs, Pam Cope, Joan Dawson, Linda DeGaeta, Janet Goad, Eda Lee Haas, Janice Hairston, Joan Hanson, Nadi Lane, Kathie Kryla, Kathy Lee, Kathleen Malarky, Kate McIntyre, Pam Pifer, Carole Rush, Marylou Sommer, and Kathleen Springer. Thanks again to the small group called "Loose Threads" for making many of the quilts you see in the photos. To all the pattern testers, thanks for your patience and persistance.

THANK YOU

Sincere thanks to Kris Krischano, who has been my proofreader through many books. Together we try to catch all the mistakes, big and small. Four eyes are better than one, and yours are talented.

DEDICATION

To our grandchildren, Taylor, Ashley, Skye, and Zev, and ones to come: Beautiful children, you bring joy to our lives. Watching you grow up makes us proud! Love from Grandma & Grandpa.

CREDITS

Photography by Terry Reed
Cover Graphics by Elizabeth Nephew

Clearview Triangle
8311 180th St. S.E.
Snohomish, WA 98296-4802

Library of Congress Control Number: 2006901564
ISBN 1-930294-05-0 and 978-1-930294-05-9

To learn more about stacked pattern repeats, read Bethany Reynolds' books, "Magic Stack 'N Whack Quilts®", "Stack 'N Whackier," and "Magic Quilts-By The Slice ."

DOUBLEDIPITY QUILTS

INTRODUCTION

A student who took my Serendipity class twice said, "I'll never make any other kind of quilt," because she enjoys the process so much. After finishing the Serendipity book, some pattern testers still wanted new patterns. I guess we weren't finished working with the designs and textures of these stacked repeat quilts. 60 blocks, 13 borders, and many new layouts later, a new book was created. I hope you enjoy it as much as I did.

THE BEST REPEAT FABRICS

It's hard to stop finding the fabrics that would be perfect for a Serendipity quilt. What is required is "six repeats of a high contrast large print." Let's consider every part of that description.

First, page four describes how to cut six repeat panels from a length of fabric. (Also see the note about Bethany Reynolds' books at the bottom of the facing page.) In fabric stores, be aware that those who are helping you cut fabric may not have taken a class that covers stacked repeats and so do not understand how to measure the fabric. Start counting your repeat panels with zero, not one, so you get six, not five, panels.

"High contrast" means the print includes areas that are very light and areas that are very dark. Black and white are as high contrast as you can get, but most quilters really like to work with color. I like a fabric with motifs floating on either a light or dark background. Some space between these motifs is desirable. If there is a lot of background between the bunches of flowers, lobsters, whatever, there could be more waste, but more choices will be possible in the cutting of your fabric shapes.

"Large print" seems to be open to a lot of interpretation judging by the fabrics that are brought to my classes. A motif that is three or four inches across will produce more variety of designs after stacking than one that is only two inches in size. Experience is the best teacher.

Beyond that, you will enjoy working with a fabric that has multiple colors in it, because each set of repeat shapes (block centers) will cause you to pull different accent fabrics, making the whole quilt more colorful and exciting.

Fabric designers choose different sizes of repeats. Some repeats can be even less than seven inches, which would not be enough to cut the shapes that you will need. In that case, double the number of repeats you buy so you have enough fabric. Ideal patterns have a short repeat of about 12-13 inches, and so you will only need to purchase about 2¼ - 2½ yards. This stack generally will provide enough stacked repeats for a whole nine-block quilt. Some elaborate prints may have a huge repeat, two feet or more. Perhaps you want to create a queen-sized quilt. Some patterns may require more waste to create attractive designs, so in that case, you might want to buy double the repeats just to make sure you have enough fabric to work with.

FINDING FABRICS

Great fabrics for stacked repeats turn up in quilt shops all the time. You will have to visit lots of quilt shops because each quilt shop has different fabrics. Beyond that, I have found great fabrics at garage sales, on the internet, and in antique stores. The advantage of garage sales and antique stores is that you get to hold the fabric in your hand. You need to be able to judge whether it's really cotton. When you crumple it in your hand do the crinkles stay? If you buy it you can test it at home by burning a snipped corner over the sink to see if it bubbles, smells like plastic burning, and leaves a hard edge - not cotton! And of course, you will want to count if six repeats are there. But you need to be a garage sale, antique store kind of person. If you hate wasting time looking at junk, it's not for you.

Antique stores and malls are where I found yardage of fabric from the Thirties for my Thirties Sampler quilt. Iowa is a great state to go antiquing in.

And I have purchased lots of fabric on Ebay. But it can be risky. It is hard to get a good feel for the scale of the print when you are only looking at a little picture on a computer monitor. This is true even though the seller may have placed a coin, etc., on the fabric. Also, I have had to return a couple of fabrics that were not cotton. By far the largest risk is how habit-forming Ebay can be. Don't start shopping online unless your powers of resistance are very strong. For all these reasons given above, if you start shopping on Ebay you are liable to end up with many fabrics you can't use for a stacked repeat project. In fact, the rule is, if you buy fabric on Ebay, you had better be prepared to **sell** fabric on Ebay.

STACKED REPEATS - PREPARING A STACK

1. **Buy six repeats (plus) of a high-contrast large print.** Wash, dry, and press selvage to selvage. (Buy a little extra to make it easier to choose the memory point.)

2. **Make a notch at the fold and tear fabric in half lengthwise.** This gives you two easy to handle lengths of six design repeats each. Set one length aside.

3. On the remaining length, along the selvage or the inside torn edge, near one cut end, **find a memory point (a particular detail, like a leaf or seashell) that will make it easy to see the six repeats.** Find the next occurrence of this detail along the same long edge, being sure there is one whole repeat between this and the previous occurrence. At this memory point, lay a 6" x 24" clear ruler across the width of the fabric section. Find more reference points across the width of the fabric, lining the ruler up perpendicular to the selvage edge. Keeping these reference points in mind and finding them again each time, cut six repeats apart with a rotary cutter, making six identical panels from the original length of fabric.

4. **Place the repeat sections on top of each other. Count the layers to make sure you have six repeats. Find a design detail again, a precise point (like the tip of a line) that is easy to see, and place a pin in it.** Work from the top down, resting your hand on the stacked layers of fabric. Put the pin point in the detail, then pull the first layer up onto the pin, placing the excess over your hand holding the pin. Repeat with the next layer, keeping the pin in the same position, only moving slightly as necessary to precisely pierce the same detail. When a detail is pierced through all layers, pin the layers together using a tight small stitch not bigger than ¼". Do this over the whole stack, using a pin every 4-6 inches in all directions. If you have a large repeat, you might have to start in the center and work out, otherwise you can work from one end to the other. During this process, you may shake and smooth the whole stack when necessary to make the layers lay flat. When the stack is pinned overall, touch with an iron here and there to mesh some fibers on the layers.

5. **Trim one cut edge of the stacked panels removing pins as necessary. Then cut** a 3½" (or according to the block pattern requirement) strip thru all the panels for triangles, or a 3¼" (or according to the block pattern requirement) strip for diamonds and flat pyramids. Again, remove the pins in that area first so the ruler lays flat and to be sure there isn't a pin in front of your rotary cutter. You may wish to waste some background fabric when cutting the strips to obtain the most beautiful design repeats.

6. **Cut diamonds or triangles from the layered strip.** (See cutting directions on pgs 7-13.) Position the diamond or triangle to get the most attractive motif on the shape, again wasting a little fabric if necessary.

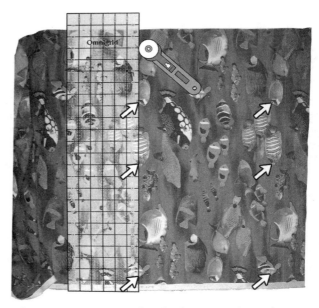

The arrows point up details showing where the printed fish pattern begins to repeat itself. Notice at the right edge where having a few extra inches of fabric allows you to choose where you want to cut the repeats.

Try Stacking With Thread

The arrow shows the leaf tip, a good precise detail to choose for stacking

Using a needle and thread: The arrow shows the needle (with a knotted thread) being inserted at the leaf tip. Then fold the top fabric up over your hand holding the needle so you can see to insert it at the same place in the next fabric panel. When all six panels are on the needle and the needle is straight up and down through all the layers, take a small tight stitch, and then a few backstitches to anchor the stitch.

ROUND ROBIN QUILTS

UFOs

You may have a stack of hexagons made from 5" triangles, since that is a popular size hexagon used in many classes. Some of the block designs in this book, and in the first Serendipity book, use 4⅞" triangles to make the center hexagon. If you have hexagons made from 5" triangles, just trim ⅛" from each triangle on the outside edge to make the smaller hexagon.

DIFFERENT ASSEMBLY METHOD

You don't have to take the 4⅞" hexagons apart to complete the block in wedges as is recommended for the patterns in this book. Instead, add the star point on three sides of the center hex, as shown at right. Then add a strip on three sides - that contains all the other parts of the design - as in the assembly diagram for the MARS block shown at right.

If you don't have any pre-sewn hexagons, you can stack and cut 4⅞" triangles and you won't have to bother trimming the edges down. And why would you want to do it that way? Because then you can play a quilt game called a round robin. In a round robin, the fabric parts of the design are passed from person to person, each adding another element until the full design is created, the quilt top is done. The author and two other quilters enjoyed a round robin with Doubledipity blocks, and the results are shown on pg. 64.

TRY A ROUND ROBIN

Each person chose the high contrast large print they wanted and made seven stacked repeat hexagons from that print. They passed on the hexagons and leftover fabric to the next person, who chose a block design and completed seven blocks using the 4⅞" hexagons. The last person made 24 setting triangles for the quilt. Then it was back to the owner to put together and add borders.

Maybe with more participants, a fourth person could put the blocks and setting triangles together, and perhaps a fifth could add a final border. It was fun to do with three anyway.

Any block that can be divided as shown in the MARS diagram below would be suitable for this assembly method. In this book, you can choose from MARS, VENUS, SWAN, and SUNSET. In addition, there are three blocks in the Serendipity book that will work, FISH, BUDDING, and SIMPLE CROCHET.

Add Three Triangles On Seperate Sides Of The Stacked Hexagon

Mars Assembly Diagram

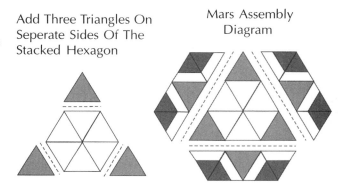

Each Of These Blocks Can Be Assembled With A Center Hex Turned Into A Triangle And Three Pieced Side Strips Added Last

Mars

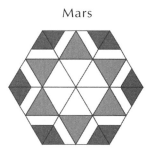

Seven Blocks To Use In A Round Robin

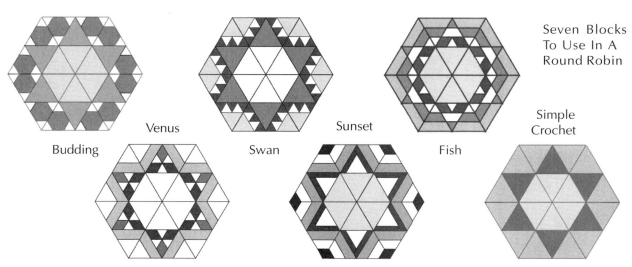

Budding

Venus

Swan

Sunset

Fish

Simple Crochet

THAT SPECIAL TOUCH

PUTTING IT ALL TOGETHER

Once your blocks are finished, you have many decisions still to make. You will choose a layout, choose your background color, choose which setting triangle you want to use. The quilts in this book show the variety of design solutions possible from a small group of quilters, some with many years of experience and some not far from the starting point. The different choices made show the variety that is possible.

DESIGNING BORDERS

The final choice many of these quilters made was to put a border on the quilt top. The author wanted to use plain borders, just strips of fabric to show these quilts could be beautiful without a lot of extra work. But then the **Winter Garden** quilt just called out for a fancy pieced border. And after the author made the DIAMOND LACE border, she was hooked on pieced borders, and all the rest of the quilts she made had to have a pieced border. Those quilts are all at least twin size, nice for naps and for hanging on a wall, but on pg. 93 some sample designs show that with a smaller quilt the border can take on even more importance and be half or two thirds of the area of the quilt. All but one (CROWN) of the borders are original designs invented for the quilts in this book.

How can you come up with a border design? You might need graph paper to fill in diamonds and triangles so you can know what pieces in what size you need to cut.

That's how I design my borders. I look for some geometric design element of the block that expresses a rhythm or a shape that I consider especially attractive, that I would like to see more of. Then I try to draw that shape on graph paper in a line like a border. Sometimes it needs to be changed for easy piecing.

But the pattern testers designed some fancy pieced borders too. One techique that often seems to be successful is to pick one pieced unit from the block, and just use that unit in the border. Pattern testers Joan Dawson and Pam Pifer were both successful with that technique. (See their quilts in the color section.) But each quilter has their own special way to come up with

new designs. What can you produce?

Even beyond pieced borders, a couple of the pattern testers added applique borders to their quilts. The organic curves of appliqué are a beautiful counterpoint to the geometry of the pieced blocks. So if you like to do some handwork, you might try an appliqué border on your quilt.

TURN A 2-ROW BLOCK INTO A 3-ROW BLOCK

Two of the quilts in this book are sampler quilts, using an assortment of blocks. If you choose to try this, you might want to mix 2-Row and 3-Row blocks in the same quilt. Do this by turning 2-Row blocks into 3-Row blocks. Any 2-Row block can be made larger by adding a flat pyramid to each wedge. This flat pyramid is cut from a 3¼" strip at the 9" line on the ruler.

When you line up the bottom of the 3¼" strip on the 9" line of the Super 60™, you'll see that the left and right edges of the ruler do not go all the way to the bottom edge of the strip. To cut such a large shape, place a straight edge ruler next to the Super 60™ as shown. Pull the Super 60™ away and cut along the straight edge. Replace the Super 60 in the correct position and place the straight edge along the other side. Pull the Super 60 away and cut along the straight edge again. You can stack the strips up to six deep. Of course, if you have the 12" triangle, you can use it instead to cut this flat pyramid.

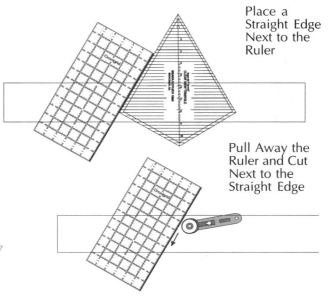

Place a Straight Edge Next to the Ruler

Pull Away the Ruler and Cut Next to the Straight Edge

VISUAL INDEX OF SHAPES TO CUT

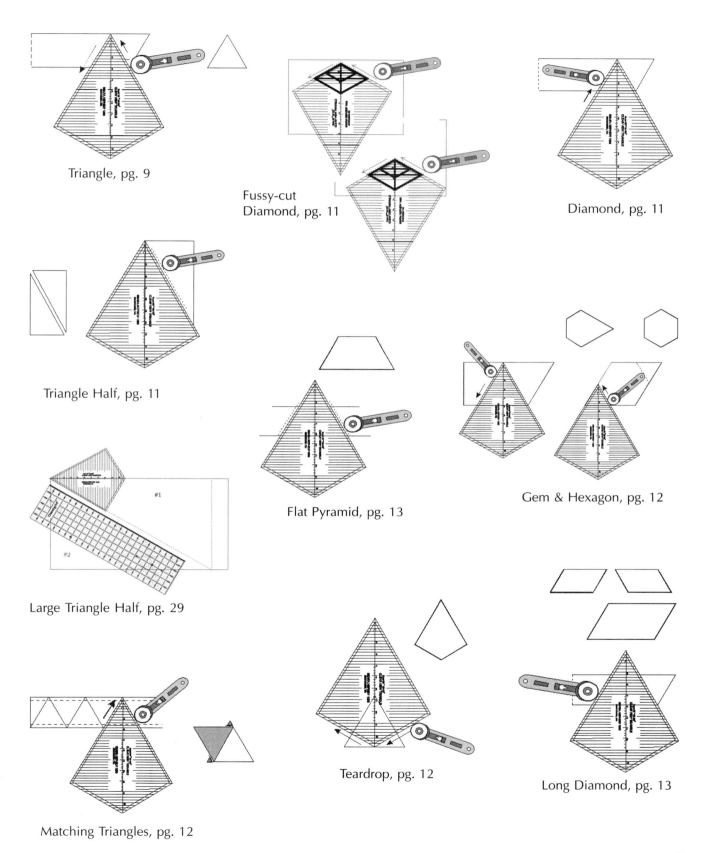

Triangle, pg. 9

Fussy-cut Diamond, pg. 11

Diamond, pg. 11

Triangle Half, pg. 11

Flat Pyramid, pg. 13

Gem & Hexagon, pg. 12

Large Triangle Half, pg. 29

Teardrop, pg. 12

Long Diamond, pg. 13

Matching Triangles, pg. 12

CUTTING DIRECTIONS

TOOLS

This book features the Super 60™. The Super 60 combines the most versatile Clearview Triangle, the 8" Mini-Pro, with the ½-diamond, so with one tool you can cut every shape needed in this book. (Sometimes a cut will need to be extended with a straight ruler to make a larger piece.)

Both the Super 60 and all the Clearview Triangles are made from ⅛" thick acrylic for use with a rotary cutter. (See pg. 112 for ordering information.) You may already own the two tools mentioned above. If so, you will not need the new tool. Just use the 8" triangle when directions refer to "the narrow end" and the ½-diamond when directions refer to "the wide end".

Besides the Super 60 or Clearview Triangles, required tools are: a rotary cutter, a mat, and a straight ruler like Omnigrid for cutting strips. Use the size of rotary cutter you prefer, although the smallest is better for cutting around curves (like cutting out clothing patterns) and the two larger sizes save muscle strain, cut faster, and tend to stay on a straight line. A 6" x 12" ruler moves less while cutting.

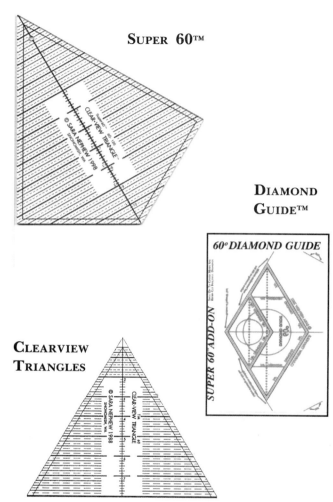

SUPER 60™

DIAMOND GUIDE™

CLEARVIEW TRIANGLES

THE DIAMOND GUIDE

This new static cling label can be added onto the wide end of the Super 60 and used as a guide for fussy-cutting two sizes of diamonds and a hexagon. Two colors are included, red and white, so the guidelines will show up well on any color of fabric. When not in use, the static cling label can be returned to its backing and kept in the package. A pattern is included.

ROTARY CUTTING AND SPEED-PIECING

These cutting methods are based on:
1. a strip of fabric;
2. a plastic 60° triangle tool with a ruled line on the perpendicular. The tool is laid on the strip in various ways, and a rotary cutter is used to cut off portions of the fabric strip. Nothing in this book is difficult to do as long as the triangle tool and the strip are kept in mind. By working just with these elements, many shapes can be cut in whatever size is desired. These shapes will all fit together to form a quilt top. The following section lists the methods for cutting the shapes used in this book.

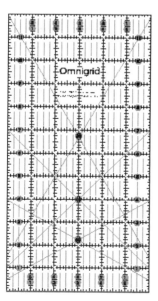

OMNIGRID™ 6" x 12"

OLFA™ CUTTER

PIECING HINTS

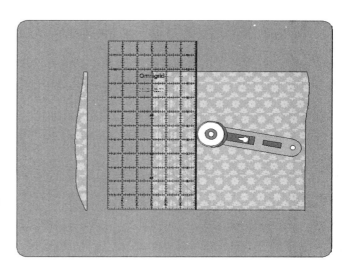

Pressed out to reduce bulk

* All my piecing is done with a ¼" seam. Check the seams occasionally until you are confident of accuracy. Be sure the seam is just inside the ¼" line rather than right on it.

* Note : More and more, I twist seams to allow seam intersections to butt up against each other, making points come together well and reducing bulk. Where a seam triangle sticks out past the fabric edge, press away from this point in both directions.

* When many seams intersect at one point, pinch the center where the seams cross, open the fabric to see how the seams are meeting and adjust as necessary. Pin to hold while stitching.

* Do not trim off the little 60° points that stick out past the fabric edge. They are very useful to help align the units for accurate sewing. Only trim them after the top is pieced if they will show through a light fabric.

* The mild bias of the 60° triangle aids in lining up seams. Pull a little if necessary. All seams are pressed to one side to make the quilt top durable. Press from the top with a wet press cloth.

TO CUT A STRIP

To cut a strip:

The first step in cutting any shape is to cut a strip. All fabric should be prewashed. 100% cotton is best.

1. Fold fabric selvage-to-selvage and press. If pressing from the selvage to the fold produces wrinkles, move the top layer of fabric left or right keeping selvages parallel, until wrinkles disappear.
2. Bring fold to selvage (folding again) and press.
3. Use the wide ruler as a right angle guide, or line up the selvages with the edge of the mat, and the ruler with the mat edge perpendicular to the selvage. Cut off the ragged or irregular edges of the fabric.
4. Cut the strip width required, using the newly trimmed fabric edge as a guide.
5. Open the strip. It should be straight, not zigzag. Adjust the ruler if necessary and trim fabric edges slightly before cutting the next strip.

Trim ragged edge from twice-folded fabric. Then begin to cut strips. Use a wide ruler (or lines on the mat) to line up cuts.

PIECES TO CUT-- TRIANGLE

To cut a triangle (3½" triangle size):

1. Cut a 3½" strip (or a strip the size of the triangle).
2. Position the narrow end of the Super 60 at one edge of the strip and the 3½" line (or the line the size of the triangle) at the other edge of the strip.
3. Rotary cut along both sides of the triangle. Move the tool along the same edge (do not flip it to the other side of the fabric strip) for the next cut. Line up the tool again as shown.
4. Cut along both sides of the triangle. Strips may be stacked up to 8 thicknesses and all cut at once.

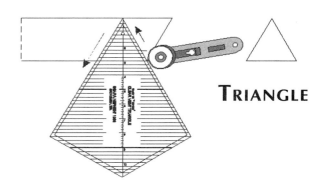

TRIANGLE

FUSSY-CUT DIAMONDS

Fussy-cut diamonds and other shapes can be chosen and cut one at a time from a single layer of fabric. The result tends to be static, tighter and more controlled than a stacked repeat. Fussy-cut repeats can create designs as precise and sparkling as a gemstone. Somewhat more fabric will be wasted by cutting only these selected designs from the whole fabric.

OR: Instead of cutting single diamonds, you can stack fabrics first, and then cut six identical, carefully chosen diamonds at the same time.

THE OLD-FASHIONED WAY

Cut a template the shape and size desired from template plastic. Position this shape on the fabric to get the most attractive design. You will most likely be wasting some fabric, but beauty is the desired result, not thrift. Mark around the template with washout marker, pencil, or a ballpoint pen that you know washes out. Cut with a scissors on the marked lines.

A FASTER WAY

The author likes to rotary cut everything, and trying to draw an outline and then cut it out got tiring very quickly! So she made a guide for rotary cutting as follows: Cut a diamond (or other shape) the size needed from a full-page computer label. Cut out a smaller diamond (or other shape) inside the first so the ¼" outline of the shape remains. Peel and stick the label diamond on the 120° end of the Super 60™ (if a triangle, on the 60° end) as a guide for centering a motif to be rotary cut. Establish a lengthwise center line by sticking on a narrow strip of the label paper down the inside center of the diamond outline. Note: When you remove the label, a little kerosene or charcoal starter fluid on a rag will clean sticker glue off without damaging the rulings. When using the rotary cutter, try not to extend the cuts farther than necessary, in order to preserve the rest of the fabric. *OR : Use the Diamond Guide™ available from Clearview Triangle for two sizes of 60° diamonds and a 3¼" hexagon. See pg. 112 for ordering information.*

GUIDE FOR TRIANGLES

Cut out triangles with the desired motif using a rotary cutter and the 60° end of the Super 60™. Use a strip of tape or computer label to show where the bottom of the triangle will be.

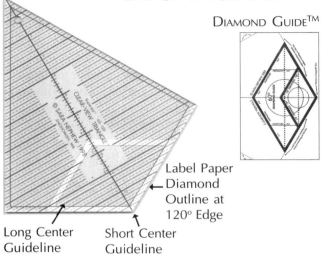

DIAMOND GUIDE™

Label Paper Diamond Outline at 120° Edge

Long Center Guideline

Short Center Guideline

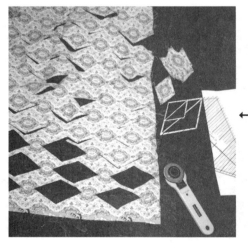

FUSSY-CUT DIAMONDS

← Super 60™ With A Handmade Diamond Guide

Example: cutting 1⅞" diamonds to make small stars. The motifs are all cut along two sides of the diamond first. Then the fabric is turned, and the other two sides are cut. Only every other motif can be used, since the cuts extend into the space in between.

Fussy-cut repeats in a diamond make a star to use in a Setting Triangle

DIAMOND

To cut a diamond (3½" triangle size) :
1. Cut a 3¼" strip (or size the directions call for).
2. Position the Super 60 (narrow end up) with one side along one edge of the strip. Cut the end of the strip to a 60° angle.
3. Reposition so the tip is at one edge of the strip and a ruled line along the other edge (same position asused to cut triangles, except the strip is ¼" narrower).
4. Rotary cut **only** along the side opposite the first cut.
5. Keep moving the tool along the same side of the strip, lining up the cut edge and the side of the tool as shown. Always cut the side opposite the first cut. (Strips may be stacked up to 8 thicknesses and all cut at once.)

FUSSY-CUT DIAMOND

To fussy-cut a diamond:
1. Center the motif in the diamond and cut along two sides of the diamond on either side of the wide angle first. Then turn the fabric and cut the other two sides. Only every other motif can be used since the cuts extend into the space in between. Try not to extend the cuts farther than necessary in order to preserve the rest of the fabric.

TRIANGLE HALF

To cut a triangle half (3½" triangle size):
Method #1
1. Cut triangles from a 4" strip.
2. Line up the side of the fabric triangle with the perpendicular line on the narrow end of the Super 60. Cut the fabric triangle in half along the edge of the tool.

Method #2
1. Cut a rectangle the height and width needed for the triangle half as given in the directions (ex. 2⅜" x 4").
2. Using the narrow end of the Super 60, bisect this rectangle from corner-to-corner diagonally. (This will produce two halves the same, rather than a left and a right. Lay the ruler from corner-to-corner to check and see if this is the shape needed. If not, lay it along the other two corners. To get left and right halves, lay two rectangles right or wrong sides together.)

LARGE TRIANGLE HALF

See the instructions and diagram on pg. 29.

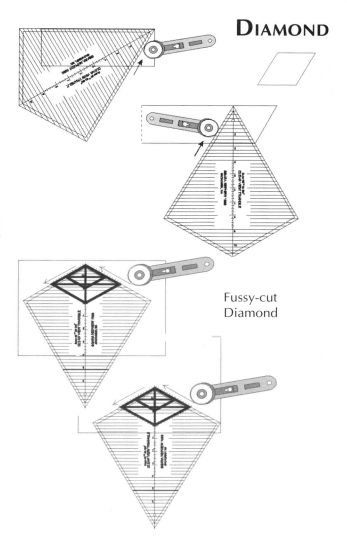

DIAMOND

Fussy-cut
Diamond

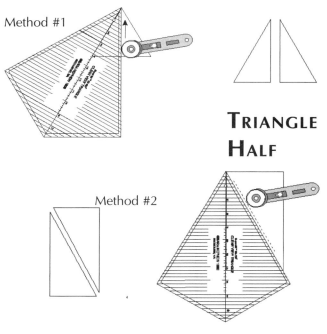

Method #1

TRIANGLE HALF

Method #2

Hexagon & Gem

To cut a hexagon:
1. Cut a 3¼" strip (6" for the whole hexagon in a setting triangle).
2. Cut 60° diamonds from the strip. (See "To cut a diamond," on pg. 11.)
3. From each end of the diamond, cut a 1⅝" triangle (3" for setting triangle hexagon).

To cut a gem shape:
Instead of cutting a hexagon from the diamond, cut only one point off, leaving the gem shape.

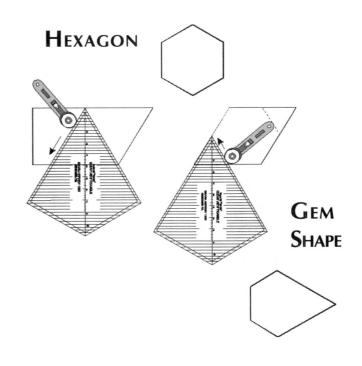

HEXAGON

GEM SHAPE

Matching Triangles

(Sandwich-Piecing uses two strips of fabric.)
To sandwich-piece a matching triangle (3½" triangle size):
1. Cut 3½" strips. (Strip width is always the same as the triangle size.) Two different fabrics are used, usually one light and one dark. Seam these strips right sides together with a ¼" seam down both the right and the left side of the pair of strips. Cut triangles from this set of strips.
2. Pull the tips of the seamed triangles apart and press.

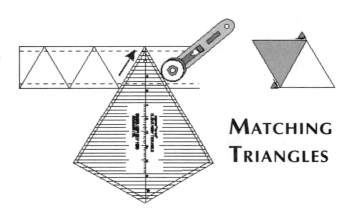

MATCHING TRIANGLES

Teardrop

To cut a teardrop (3½" triangle size):
Method #1
1. Cut triangles from strip size given in the directions.
2. Position the Super 60 on the triangle upside down and centered, with the perpendicular line on the top point of the triangle, the other two triangle points lined up evenly with one of the rulings, and the wide angle just at or inside the bottom edge as shown. Cut excess from the base of the teardrop.

Method #2 (Using a Clearview Triangle)
1. Cut triangles from a strip.
2. Measure the base of these triangles and find the center or half measurement.
3. Lay the perpendicular of the triangle tool along the base of the fabric triangle with the point at center. Rotary cut this wedge off. Reverse the tool and cut off the other wedge.

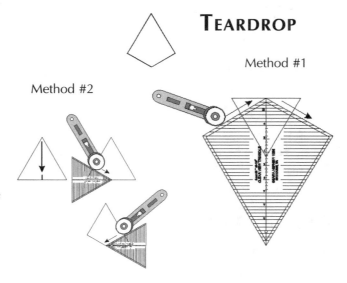

TEARDROP

Method #1

Method #2

LONG DIAMOND

To cut a long diamond (3½" triangle size):
1. Cut strip width as required in the pattern.
2. Trim one end of the strip to a 60° angle.
3. Place the Super 60 over the fabric strip as shown. Set the bottom edge of the strip at the measurement given in the pattern. Cut the side opposite the first cut.

Or:
1. After cutting the correct width strip, trim it to a 60° angle as in #1 and #2 above.
2. Use a straight ruler to cut the correct width parallel to the angled end.

Long diamonds do have a reverse of their shape. Check carefully to be sure you are cutting them in the direction required by the pattern.

FLAT PYRAMID

To cut a flat pyramid (3½" triangle size):
1. Cut a 3¼" strip (or size the directions call for).
2. Place the narrow end of the Super 60 over the fabric strip, lining up the bottom edge of the strip at the measurement given in the pattern (often 6¼"). Cut on both sides of the tool.
3. Turn the Super 60 and cut the next flat pyramid from the other side of the strip to save fabric.

STRIP-PIECED TRIANGLES

Some of these designs can be speeded up by sewing strips together first, and then cutting triangles from the strip. A few piecing tips will help to improve accuracy and and give a look of crisp precision. Of course, careful cutting of the strips is important. In addition:
1. Sometimes it helps to always begin sewing at the same edge of the strip set.
2. Press to the dark if possible.
3. Press across the strip set, from the back, and pull it as wide as possible to make sure there is no fabric folded into the seam.
4. Then press the strip from the front, lengthwise, pulling to make the set of strips straight. Use a wet press cloth if you wish.

LONG DIAMOND

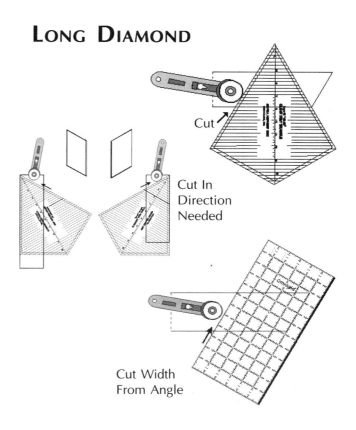

Cut

Cut In Direction Needed

Cut Width From Angle

FLAT PYRAMID

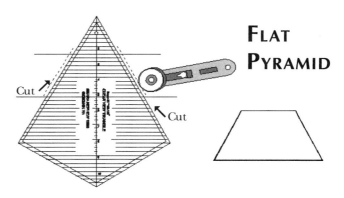

Cut

Cut

STRIP-PIECED LONG DIAMONDS & REVERSE

Cut a light and a dark 3¼" strip. Sew together lengthwise. Fold right sides together or make two strip sets and place right sides together, do not butt the seams, but place light to light, and dark to dark. Trim the strip set to a 60° angle, then cut 1⅞" sections from the strip set. Check the 60° angle often.

VISUAL INDEX OF 2-ROW SERENDIPITY BLOCKS
In Alphabetical Order

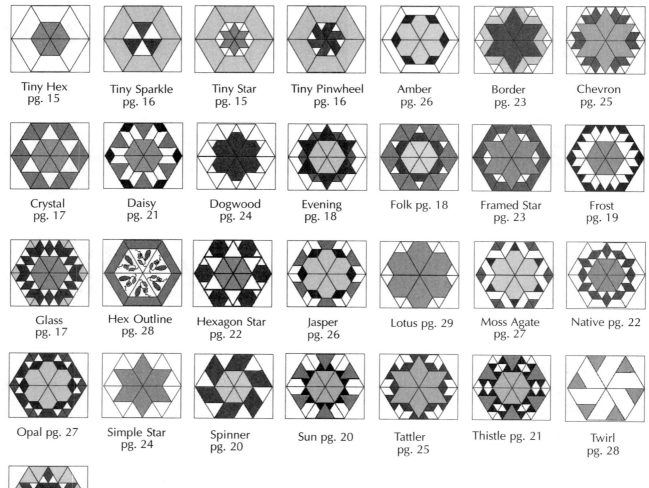

Tiny Hex
pg. 15

Tiny Sparkle
pg. 16

Tiny Star
pg. 15

Tiny Pinwheel
pg. 16

Amber
pg. 26

Border
pg. 23

Chevron
pg. 25

Crystal
pg. 17

Daisy
pg. 21

Dogwood
pg. 24

Evening
pg. 18

Folk pg. 18

Framed Star
pg. 23

Frost
pg. 19

Glass
pg. 17

Hex Outline
pg. 28

Hexagon Star
pg. 22

Jasper
pg. 26

Lotus pg. 29

Moss Agate
pg. 27

Native pg. 22

Opal pg. 27

Simple Star
pg. 24

Spinner
pg. 20

Sun pg. 20

Tattler
pg. 25

Thistle pg. 21

Twirl
pg. 28

Window
pg. 19

CHOOSE FROM 29
DIFFERENT BLOCKS

3½" CENTER TRIANGLE, PGS. 17-22
3¼" CENTER DIAMOND, PGS. 23-27
CENTER FLAT PYRAMID, PG. 28
4⅞" CENTER TRIANGLE, PGS. 28-29

HINT: THE SMALLER CENTER REPEAT SHAPES ARE EASIER TO WORK WITH, BUT LARGER SHAPES CAN PRODUCE EXCEPTIONAL RESULTS.

TINY HEX

1. Cut for one block:

1.	6	center*	3½"	triangle
2.	6	light	6¼"	flat pyramid
				from 3¼" strip

TINY HEX BLOCK

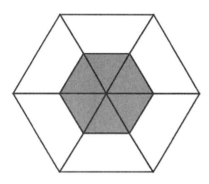

2. Sew one light 6¼" flat pyramid and a center 3½" triangle into a wedge as shown. Make six of these.

3. Sew the wedges three and three and sew across the middle to make a hexagon block.

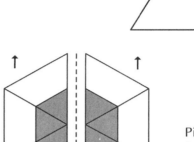

One Wedge

Piecing Diagram
Press seams away
from center
Pinch and pin center

TINY STAR

All cutting is based on the 3½" triangle size.

1. Cut for one block:

1.	6	center*	1⅞"	diamond
2.	12	light	2⅛"	triangle
3.	6	light	6¼"	flat pyramid
				from 3¼" strip

2. Sew two 2⅛" triangles onto a 1⅞" diamond to make a pieced triangle as shown. Add one light 6¼" flat pyramid to create a wedge . Make six of these.

3. Sew the wedges three and three and sew across the middle to make a hexagon block.

Pieced Triangle

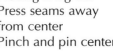

*Repeat ← Fabric

TINY STAR BLOCK

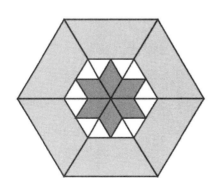

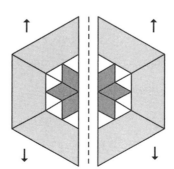

Piecing Diagram
Press seams away
from center
Pinch and pin center

15

TINY PINWHEEL

All cutting is based on the 3½" triangle size.

1. Cut for one block:

1.	6	light	2⅛"	triangle
2.	6	dark	3½"	flat pyramid
				from 1⅞" strip
3.	6	light	6¼"	flat pyramid
				from 3¼" strip

2. Sew a light 2⅛" triangle and a center 3½" flat pyramid into a pieced triangle as shown. Add a 6¼" flat pyramid to make one wedge. Make six of these.

3. Sew the wedges three and three and sew across the middle to make a hexagon block.

TINY PINWHEEL BLOCK

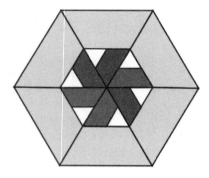

Repeat * Fabric →
Pieced Triangle

One Wedge

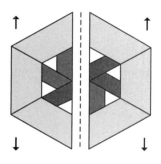

Piecing Diagram
Press seams away
from center
Pinch and pin center

TINY SPARKLE

All cutting is based on the 3½" triangle size.

1. Cut for one block:

1.	3 dark and 3 light	3½"	triangle
2.	6	light	6¼"	flat pyramid
				from 3¼" strip

2. Sew a light 3½" triangle onto a light 6¼" flat pyramid to create a wedge. Make three of these. Make three with a dark triangle.

3. Sew the wedges alternately three and three and sew across the middle as shown to make a hexagon block.

TINY SPARKLE BLOCK

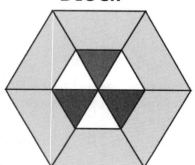

Wedge Piecing Diagram

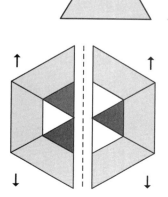

Piecing Diagram
Press seams away
from center
Pinch and pin center

CRYSTAL

1. Cut for one block:

1.	6 center❉	3½"	triangle
2.	6 light		
3.	12 medium		

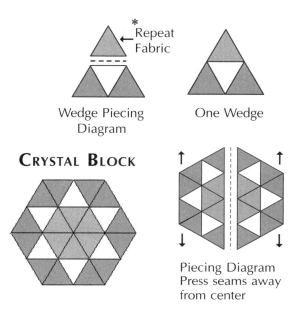

Directions:
2. Assemble a center triangle, a light triangle, and two medium triangles into a wedge as shown. Make six of these. Sew the wedges three and three and sew across the middle to make a hexagon block.

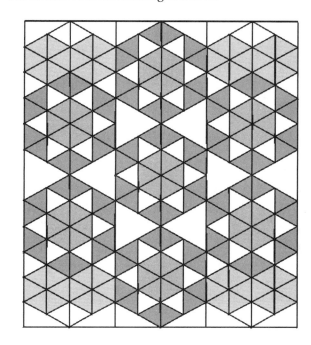

GLASS

All cutting is based on the 3½" triangle size.

1. Cut for one block:

1.	6 center❉	3½"	triangle
2.	24 light, 12 medium	2⅛"	triangle
3.	18 dark	1⅞"	diamond

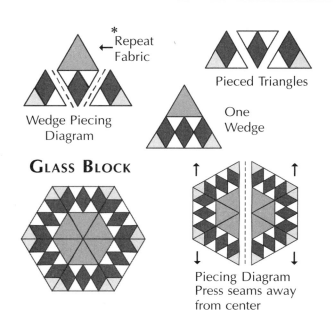

Directions:
2. From two light 2⅛" triangles and a dark 1⅞" diamond, assemble a pieced triangle. Make two more with a medium triangle on opposite corners. Add a center 3½" triangle and assemble into a wedge as shown. Make six of these. Sew the wedges three and three and sew across the middle to make a hexagon block.

EVENING

All cutting is based on the 3½" triangle size.

1. Cut for one block:

1.	6 center*	3½"	triangle
2.	6 dark		
3.	12 stripped		

Directions:

2. Cut a light and a medium 2⅛" strip and sew together lengthwise. Cut 3¾" triangles from this set of strips. Cut ¼" from the bottom of each stripped triangle. (You will get both dark and light-based triangles. Use both or only one kind.) Assemble into a wedge as shown. Make six of these. Sew the wedges three and three and sew across the middle to make a hexagon block.

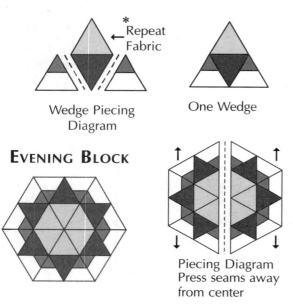

← Repeat Fabric

Wedge Piecing Diagram

One Wedge

EVENING BLOCK

Piecing Diagram
Press seams away
from center

FOLK

All cutting is based on the 3½" triangle size.

1. Cut for one block:

1.	6 center*	3½"	triangle
2.	6 stripped		
3.	12 medium		

Directions:

2. Cut a light and a dark 2⅛" strip and sew together lengthwise. Cut 3¾" triangles from this set of strips. Cut ¼" from the bottom of each stripped triangle. (You will get both dark and light-based triangles. Use both or only one kind.) Assemble into a wedge as shown. Make six of these. Sew the wedges three and three and sew across the middle to make a hexagon block.

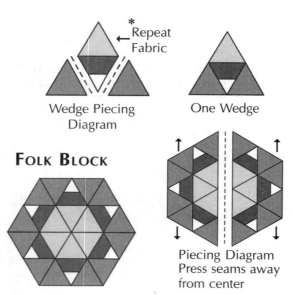

← Repeat Fabric

Wedge Piecing Diagram

One Wedge

FOLK BLOCK

Piecing Diagram
Press seams away
from center

WINDOW

All cutting is based on the 3½" triangle size.

1. Cut for one block:

1.	6 center*	3½"	triangle
2.	12 light	2⅛"	triangle
3.	6 dark	1⅞"	diamond
4.	12 medium	3½"	triangle

Directions:

2. From a dark 1⅞" diamond and two light 2⅛" triangles, make a pieced triangle as shown. Assemble a center triangle, a pieced triangle, and two medium triangles into a wedge as shown. Make six of these. Sew the wedges three and three and sew across the middle to make a hexagon block.

Pieced Triangle

Wedge Piecing Diagram

*Repeat Fabric

One Wedge

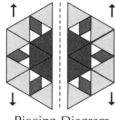

WINDOW BLOCK

Piecing Diagram
Press seams away from center

FROST

All cutting is based on the 3½" triangle size.

1. Cut for one block:

1.	6 center*, 6 med.	3½"	triangle
2.	12 dark	2⅛"	triangle
3.	6 light	1⅞"	diamond

Directions:

2. From two dark 2⅛" triangles and a light 1⅞" diamond, assemble a pieced triangle as shown. Add a center triangle and a medium triangle to make one wedge as shown. Make six of these. Sew the wedges three and three and sew across the middle to make a hexagon block.

Pieced Triangle

Wedge Piecing Diagram

*Repeat Fabric

One Wedge

FROST BLOCK

Piecing Diagram
Press seams away from center

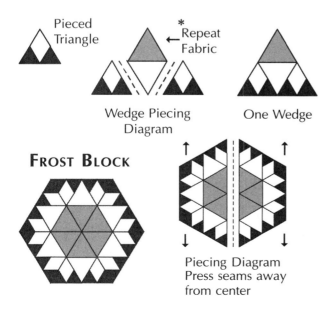

19

SPINNER

1. Cut for one block:

1.	6 center*	3½"	triangle
2.	6 dark	3¼"	diamond
3.	6 light	3½"	triangle

Directions:
2. Assemble a center triangle, a light triangle, and a dark diamond into a wedge as shown. Make six of these. Sew the wedges three and three and sew across the middle to make a hexagon block.

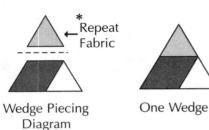

Wedge Piecing
Diagram

One Wedge

SPINNER BLOCK

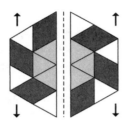

Piecing Diagram
Press seams away
from center

SUN

All cutting is based on the 3½" triangle size.

1. Cut for one block:

1.	6 center*, 6 medium	3½"	triangle
2.	6 dark	2⅛"	triangle
3.	12 light	3½"	flat pyramid from 1⅞" strip

Directions:
2. Assemble a center triangle a medium triangle, two dark 2⅛" triangles, and 2 flat pyramids into a wedge as shown. Make six of these. Sew the wedges three and three and sew across the middle to make a hexagon block.

Wedge Piecing
Diagram

One Wedge

SUN BLOCK

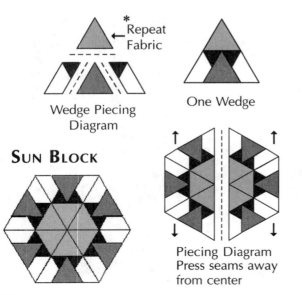

Piecing Diagram
Press seams away
from center

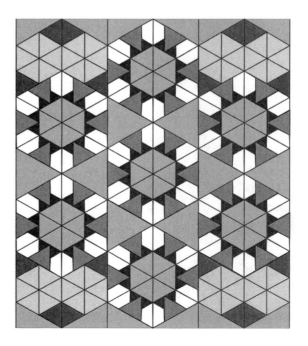

20

DAISY

All cutting is based on the 3½" triangle size.

1. Cut for one block:

1.	6 center*, 6 medium	3½"	triangle
2.	12 dark	2⅛"	triangle
3.	12 light	3½"	flat pyramid from 1⅞" strip

Directions:
2. Assemble a center triangle, a medium triangle, two dark triangles, and two flat pyramids into a wedge as shown. Make six of these. Sew the wedges three and three and sew across the middle to make a hexagon block.

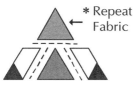
Wedge Piecing Diagram

One Wedge

DAISY BLOCK

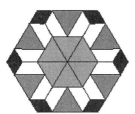

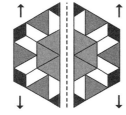
Piecing Diagram
Press seams away from center

THISTLE

All cutting is based on the 3½" triangle size.

1. Cut for one block:

1.	6 center*, 6 medium	3½"	triangle
2.	24 dark , 24 light**	2⅛"	triangle
**or sandwich-piece 24 pairs of 2⅛" matching triangles			

Directions:
2. Use two sets each of 2⅛" matching triangles to make pieced strips A and B. Add a center and a medium triangle as shown to make one wedge . Make six of these. Sew the wedges three and three and sew across the middle to make a hexagon block.

Pieced Strip A   Pieced Strip B

Wedge Piecing Diagram

One Wedge

THISTLE BLOCK

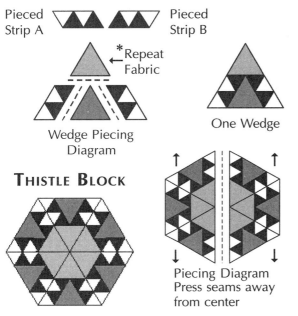

Piecing Diagram
Press seams away from center

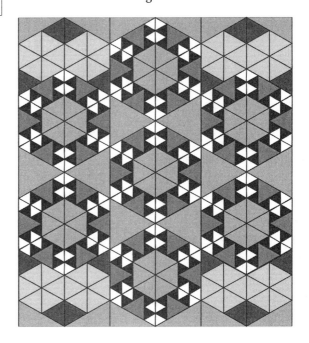

HEXAGON STAR

Directions:

2. Assemble a hexagon from six repeat 3½" triangles. Add three light 3½" triangles to make a center triangle as shown. Use two hexagons, four light 2⅛" triangles, and one light 3½" triangle to make a pieced strip. Make three of these. Sew the strips on the three sides of the center triangle to make a hexagon block.

1. Cut for one block:

1.	6 center*	3½"	triangle
2.	6 light		
3.	12 light	2⅛"	
4.	6 dark	3¼"	hexagon

Pieced Strip

← Repeat Fabric

Center Triangle Piecing Diagram

HEXAGON STAR BLOCK

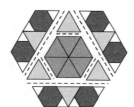

Piecing Diagram

NATIVE

All cutting is based on the 3½" triangle size.

1. Cut for one block:

1.	6 center*	3½"	triangle
2.	12 light	2⅛"	triangle
3.	6 dark	1⅞"	diamond

Directions:

2. From two light 2⅛" triangles and a dark 1⅞" diamond assemble a pieced triangle as shown. Cut a light and a dark 2⅛" strip and sew together lengthwise. Cut 3¾" triangles from this set of strips. Cut ¼" from the bottom of each stripped triangle. (You will get both dark and light-based triangles. Use both or only one kind.) Add a center triangle to one pieced and two stripped triangles to make one wedge as shown. Make six of these. Sew the wedges three and three and sew across the middle to make a hexagon block.

← Repeat Fabric

Wedge Piecing Diagram

Pieced Triangle

Stripped Triangle

One Wedge

NATIVE BLOCK

Piecing Diagram
Press seams away from center

FRAMED STAR

1. Cut for one block:

1.	6 center*	3¼"	diamond

Directions:
2. Cut a light and a dark 2⅛" strip and sew together lengthwise. Cut 3¾" triangles from this set of strips. Cut ¼" from the bottom of each stripped triangle. (You will get both dark and light-based triangles. Use both or only one kind.)

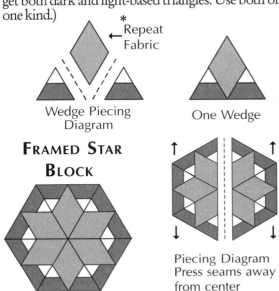

Repeat Fabric

Wedge Piecing Diagram

One Wedge

FRAMED STAR BLOCK

↑ Piecing Diagram Press seams away from center ↑

3. Assemble a center diamond and two stripped triangles into a wedge as shown. Make six of these. Sew the wedges three and three and sew across the middle to make a hexagon block.

BORDER

1. Cut for one block:

1.	6 center*	3¼"	diamond

Directions:
2. Cut a light and a dark 2⅛" strip and sew together lengthwise. Cut 3¾" triangles from this set of strips. Cut ¼" from the bottom of each stripped triangle. (You will get both dark and light-based triangles. Use both or only one kind.)

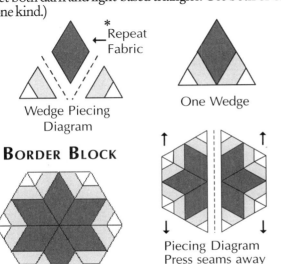

Repeat Fabric

Wedge Piecing Diagram

One Wedge

BORDER BLOCK

↑ Piecing Diagram Press seams away from center ↑

3. Assemble a center diamond and two stripped triangles into a wedge as shown. Make six of these. Sew the wedges three and three and sew across the middle to make a hexagon block.

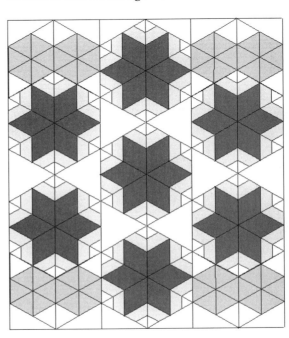

DOGWOOD

1. Cut for one block:

1.	6 center*	3¼"	gem
2.	6 light	2⅛"	triangle
3.	12 light	3½"	triangle

Directions:

2. Make a center* gem shape by cutting 1⅝" off one end of a 3¼" diamond. Sew on a light 2⅛" triangle to complete the pieced diamond. Add two light 3½" triangles to make one wedge. Make six of these. Sew the wedges three and three and sew across the middle to complete the hexagon block.

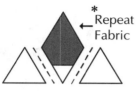

Wedge Piecing Diagram

One Wedge

DOGWOOD BLOCK

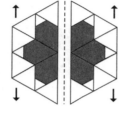

Piecing Diagram
Press seams away from center

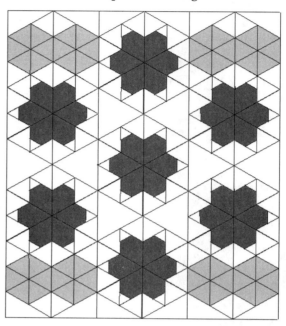

SIMPLE STAR

1. Cut for one block:

1.	6 center*	3¼"	diamond
2.	6 light	3½"	triangle

Directions:

2. Assemble a center diamond and two light triangles into a wedge as shown. Make six of these. Sew the wedges three and three and sew across the middle to make a hexagon block.

Wedge Piecing Diagram

One Wedge

SIMPLE STAR BLOCK

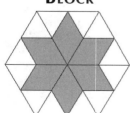

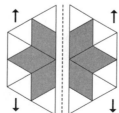

Piecing Diagram
Press seams away from center

CHEVRON

All cutting is based on the 3½" triangle size.

1. Cut for one block:

1.	6 center*	3¼"	diamond
2.	24 light	2⅛"	triangle
3.	12 dark	1⅞"	diamond

Directions:
2. From two light 2⅛" triangles and a dark 1⅞" diamond assemble a pieced triangle as shown. Assemble a center diamond and two pieced triangles into a wedge as shown. Make six of these. Sew the wedges three and three and sew across the middle to make a hexagon block.

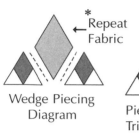

Wedge Piecing Diagram

Pieced Triangle

One Wedge

CHEVRON BLOCK

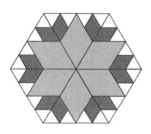

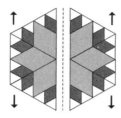

Piecing Diagram
Press seams away from center

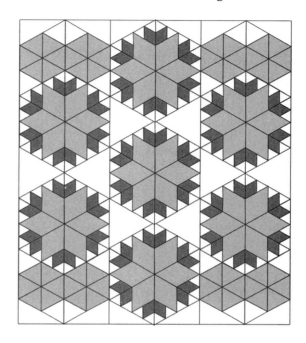

TATTLER

All cutting is based on the 3½" triangle size.

1. Cut for one block:

1.	6 center*	3¼"	diamond
2.	24 dark	2⅛"	triangle
3.	12 light	1⅞"	diamond

Directions:
2. From two dark 2⅛" triangles and a light 1⅞" diamond assemble a pieced triangle as shown. Assemble a center diamond and two pieced triangles into a wedge as shown. Make six of these. Sew the wedges three and three and sew across the middle to make a hexagon block.

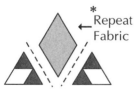

Pieced Triangle

Wedge Piecing Diagram

One Wedge

TATTLER BLOCK

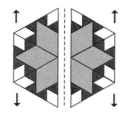

Piecing Diagram
Press seams away from center

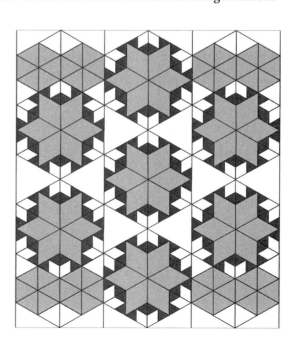

AMBER

All cutting is based on the 3½" triangle size.

1. Cut for one block:

1.	6 center*	3¼"	diamond
2.	12 dark	2⅛"	triangle
3.	6 light	6¼"	flat pyramid from a 1⅞" strip

Directions:

2. Cut a 1⅝" triangle from one end of the center* diamond. Then sew two dark 2⅛" triangles on two corners of the resulting gem shape to assemble a pieced triangle as shown. Add a flat pyramid to make a wedge as shown. Make six of these. Sew the wedges three and three and sew across the middle to make a hexagon block.

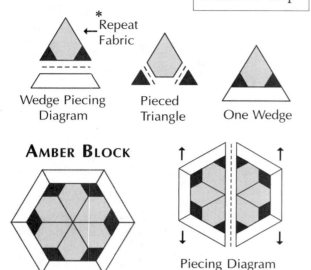

Repeat Fabric

Wedge Piecing Diagram

Pieced Triangle

One Wedge

AMBER BLOCK

Piecing Diagram
Press seams away from center

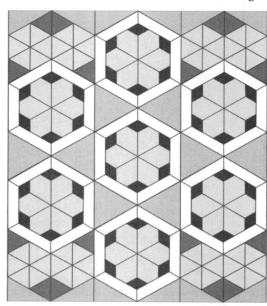

JASPER

All cutting is based on the 3½" triangle size.

1. Cut for one block:

1.	6 center*	3¼"	diamond
2.	12 dark	2⅛"	triangle
3.	12 light	1⅞"	diamond
4.	6 medium	3½"	flat pyramid from a 1⅞" strip

Directions:

2. Cut a 1⅝" triangle from one end of the center* diamond. Then sew two dark 2⅛" triangles on two corners of the resulting gem shape to assemble a pieced triangle as shown. Add a strip made from two light 1⅞" diamonds and a medium flat pyramid to make a wedge as shown. Make six of these. Sew the wedges three and three and sew across the middle to make a hexagon block.

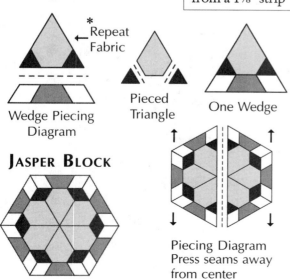

Repeat Fabric

Wedge Piecing Diagram

Pieced Triangle

One Wedge

JASPER BLOCK

Piecing Diagram
Press seams away from center

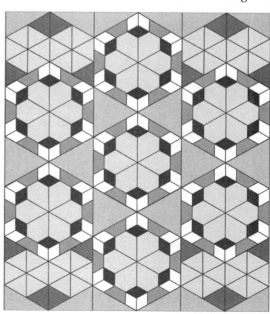

OPAL

1. Cut for one block:

1.	6 center*	3¼"	diamond
2.	12 dark	2⅛"	triangle
3.	12 light/dark	2⅛"	matching triangle
4.	6 dark	3½"	flat pyramid from a 1⅞" strip

Directions:

2. Cut a 1⅝" triangle from one end of the center* diamond. Then sew two dark 2⅛" triangles on two corners of the resulting gem shape to assemble a pieced triangle as shown. Add a strip made from two matching triangles and a dark flat pyramid to make a wedge as shown. Make six of these. Sew the wedges three and three and sew across the middle to make a hexagon block.

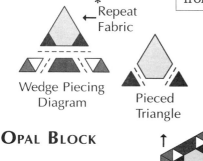

* ← Repeat Fabric

Wedge Piecing Diagram

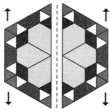

Pieced Triangle

One Wedge

OPAL BLOCK

Piecing Diagram
Press seams away from center

MOSS AGATE

All cutting is based on the 3½" triangle size.

1. Cut for one block:

1.	6 center*	3¼"	diamond
2.	6 dark	2⅛"	triangle
3.	6 stripped	3½"	triangle

Directions:

2. Cut a 1⅝" triangle from one end of the center* diamond. Then sew one dark 2⅛" triangle on to reassemble a diamond as shown. Sew two 2⅛" strips together lengthwise. Cut 3½" triangles from this set of strips. Add two stripped triangles to the center diamond to make a wedge as shown. Make six of these. Sew the wedges three and three and sew across the middle to make a hexagon block.

* ← Repeat Fabric

Wedge Piecing Diagram

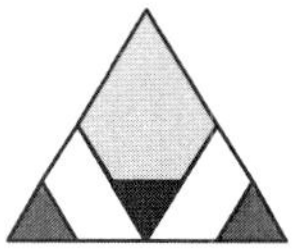

One Wedge

MOSS AGATE BLOCK

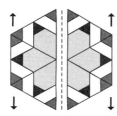

Piecing Diagram
Press seams away from center

TWIRL

All cutting is based on the 3½" triangle size.

1. Cut for one block:

1.	6 light	3½"	triangle
2.	6 center*	6¼"	flat pyramid (3¼" strip)

Directions:

2. Assemble a light triangle and a center* 6¼" flat pyramid into a wedge as shown. Make six of these. Sew the wedges three and three and sew across the middle to make a hexagon block.

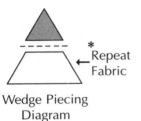

Wedge Piecing Diagram

One Wedge

TWIRL BLOCK

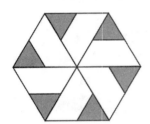

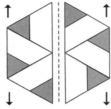

Piecing Diagram
Press seams away
from center

HEX OUTLINE

All cutting is based on the 3½" triangle size.

1. Cut for one block:

1.	6 center*	4⅞"	triangle
2.	6 medium	6¼"	flat pyramid from a 1⅞" strip

Directions:

2. Assemble a center triangle and a flat pyramid into a wedge as shown. Make six of these. Sew the wedges three and three and sew across the middle to make a hexagon block.

Wedge Piecing
Diagram

One Wedge

HEX OUTLINE BLOCK

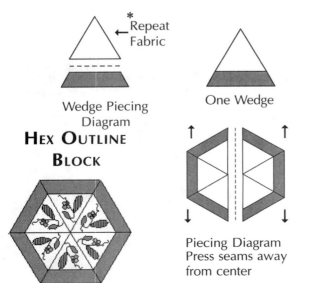

Piecing Diagram
Press seams away
from center

LOTUS

All cutting is based on the 3½" triangle size.

1. Cut for one block:

1.	6 center*	4⅛"	gem
2.	12 light	2⅝"	triangle

Directions:
2. Assemble a gem shape (4⅛" diamond, trim off a 2" triangle) and two light 2⅝" triangles into a wedge as shown. Make six. Sew the wedges three and three and sew across the middle to make a hexagon block.

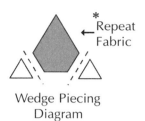

*Repeat Fabric

Wedge Piecing Diagram

One Wedge

LOTUS BLOCK

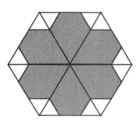

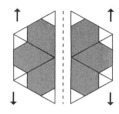

Piecing Diagram
Press seams away from center

CUTTING A LARGE TRIANGLE HALF

Some quilt layouts square up the four corners of the design with a very large triangle half. You could cut a large triangle and cut it in half down the middle. Or another approach is to use a selvage-to-selvage piece of fabric folded selvages together. This has to be at least as long as the height of the large triangle that would be cut in half. At one end place the top point of the Super 60™ or 8" or 12" triangle, lining it up at the center perpendicular line (30° angle, see diagram at right). Place a long straightedge next to the Super 60™ to extend the cut. Move it right in till it touches the tool. Then remove the triangle ruler. (You may wish to check the other end of the cut with the top of the Super 60™ to be sure it is an accurate 60° angle.) Rotary cut along the straightedge. Trim off any excess height of fabric. Then cut along the fold. This will give you two large triangle halves (#1), a right and a left. Then the other half of the fabric rectangle (#2) will give you the other two triangle halves after trimming the selvages.

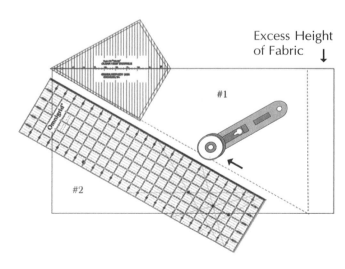

Excess Height of Fabric ↓

#1

#2

If a selvage-to-selvage fold is too narrow to cut the large triangle half you need, open the fabric and fold across the complete width. Though I have never needed a piece that large.

Visual Index Of 3-Row Blocks
In Alphabetical Order

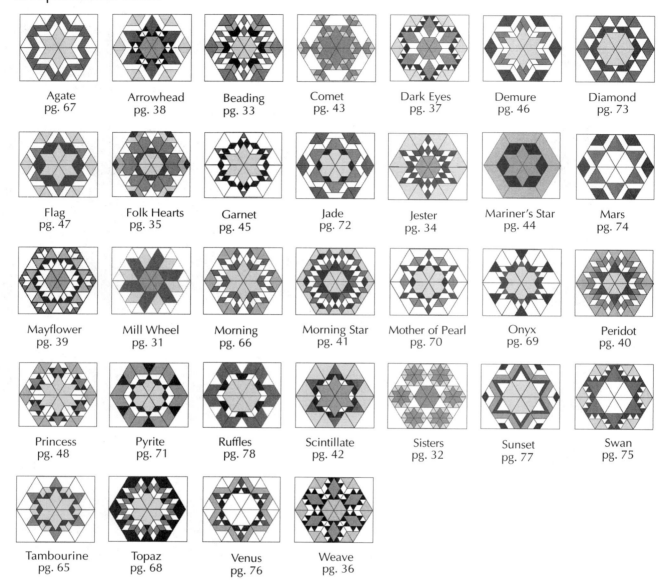

Agate
pg. 67

Arrowhead
pg. 38

Beading
pg. 33

Comet
pg. 43

Dark Eyes
pg. 37

Demure
pg. 46

Diamond
pg. 73

Flag
pg. 47

Folk Hearts
pg. 35

Garnet
pg. 45

Jade
pg. 72

Jester
pg. 34

Mariner's Star
pg. 44

Mars
pg. 74

Mayflower
pg. 39

Mill Wheel
pg. 31

Morning
pg. 66

Morning Star
pg. 41

Mother of Pearl
pg. 70

Onyx
pg. 69

Peridot
pg. 40

Princess
pg. 48

Pyrite
pg. 71

Ruffles
pg. 78

Scintillate
pg. 42

Sisters
pg. 32

Sunset
pg. 77

Swan
pg. 75

Tambourine
pg. 65

Topaz
pg. 68

Venus
pg. 76

Weave
pg. 36

32 Blocks To Choose From

3½" Center Triangle, pgs. 31-41
3¼" Center Diamond, pgs. 42-48 & 65-72
4⅞" Center Triangle, pgs. 73-78

Mill Wheel

1. Cut for one block:

1.	6	center*	3½"	triangle
2.	18	light	3½"	triangle
3.	6	medium	3¼"	diamond
4.	18	dark	6¼"	flat pyramid from 3¼" strip

All cutting is based on the 3½" triangle size.

Directions:

2. Sew one medium 3¼" diamond and two light 3½" triangles into a pieced triangle as shown. Sew one flat pyramid, one light triangle, and one center* triangle into a pieced strip. Assemble into one wedge as shown. Make six of these.

3. Sew the wedges three and three and sew across the middle to make a hexagon block.

Pieced Strip

Pieced Triangle

*Repeat Fabric

* Repeat Fabric

Wedge Piecing Diagram

One Wedge

MILL WHEEL BLOCK

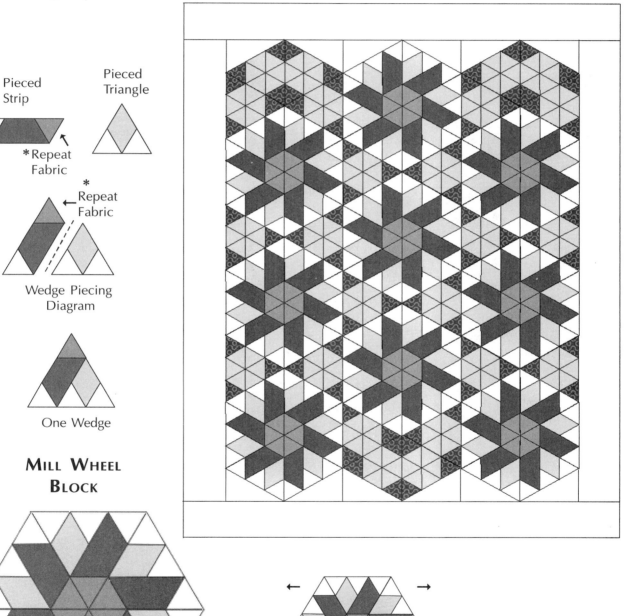

PIECING DIAGRAM
Press seams away from center
Pinch and pin center

31

SISTERS

Directions:

2. Sew a 1⅞" diamond and two 2⅛" triangles into a pieced triangle as shown. Make six of these. Sew three and three and sew across the middle, matching center points, to make a six-pointed star. Make six of these.

3. Sew the center stacked repeats into a hexagon. Add light 3½" triangles on three sides to make the center triangle. Use stars and light 3½" triangles to make three sections as shown. Sew on, in order, to complete the hexagon block.

3½" TRIANGLE CENTER REPEAT* FABRIC
All cutting is based on the 3½" triangle size.

1. Cut for one block:

1.	6	center*	3½"	triangle
2.	12	light	3½"	triangle
3.	36	medium	1⅞"	diamond
4.	72	light	2⅛"	triangle

Pieced Triangle

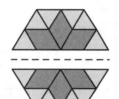

Sew Three & Three & Across The Center

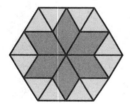

One Small Star

SISTERS BLOCK

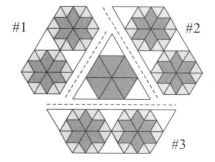

#1 #2 #3

PIECING DIAGRAM
Sew Three Sections Onto Center Triangle In Order As Shown

BEADING

Directions:

2. Sew one light and one medium 1⅞" strip together lengthwise. Cut the end to a 60° angle and cut 1⅞" sections from this set of strips. Sew two sections together into a pieced diamond as shown below. Make six of these.

3. Sew one dark and one medium 1⅞" strip together lengthwise. Make another set of strips the same and place both right sides together.. Cut the end to a 60° angle and cut 1⅞" sections from these sets of strips. Add a light 2⅛" triangle to make a pieced strip and its reverse as shown.

4. Assemble according to the diagram.

1. Cut for one block:

1.	6 center*	3½"	triangle
2.	6 medium	3½"	triangle
3.	12 light	2⅛"	triangle
4.	12 light	3½"	flat pyramid from 1⅞" strip

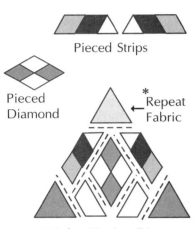

Pieced Strips

Pieced Diamond

← *Repeat Fabric

Wedge Piecing Diagram

One Wedge

BEADING BLOCK

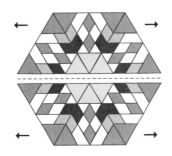

PIECING DIAGRAM
Press seams away from center
Pinch and pin center

JESTER

All cutting is based on the 3½" triangle size.

1. Cut for one block:

1.	6	center*	3½"	triangle
2.	12	dark	1⅞"	diamond
3.	12	light	2⅛"	triangle
4.	12	medium	4⅞"	triangle

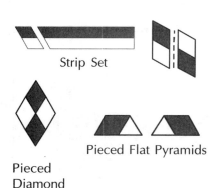

Strip Set

Pieced Diamond

Pieced Flat Pyramids

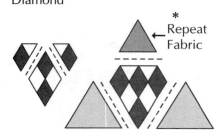

*
← Repeat Fabric

Wedge Piecing Diagram

One Wedge

JESTER BLOCK

3½" TRIANGLE CENTER REPEAT* FABRIC

Directions:

2. Sew a light and dark 1⅞" strip together lengthwise. Trim the end to a 60° angle, and cut 1⅞" sections from this set of strips, checking the angle often. Sew two sections together as shown to make a pieced diamond. Make six. Sew a 2⅛" triangle to a 1⅞" diamond as shown to make a pieced flat pyramid. Make six. Make six reverse.

3. From a pieced diamond, two flat pyramids, a center triangle and two 4⅞" triangles, assemble one wedge as shown. Make six. Sew the wedges together into two sets of three. Pinch and pin and sew all the way across to join the two halves and complete the hexagon block.

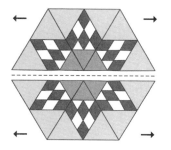

PIECING DIAGRAM
Press seams away from center
Pinch and pin center

FOLK HEARTS

Directions:

2. Cut a light and dark 2⅛" strip and sew them together lengthwise. Cut 3¾" triangles from this set of strips. Cut off a ¼" strip from the bottom of each of these stripped triangles. You will need 12 light-based and 6 dark-based triangles for each block.

3. Make a gem shape by cutting a 1⅝" triangle off one end of a 3¼" diamond. Sew on a light 2⅛" triangle to make a pieced diamond. Make two. Assemble this with a center triangle, and two light-based and one dark-based stripped triangles, and one light triangle as shown to make one wedge. Make six of these.

4. Sew the wedges three and three and sew across the middle to complete the hexagon block.

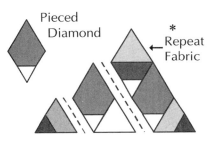

Pieced Diamond

* ← Repeat Fabric

Wedge Piecing Diagram

One Wedge

FOLK HEARTS BLOCK

3½" TRIANGLE CENTER REPEAT* FABRIC
All cutting is based on the 3½" triangle size.

1. Cut for one block:

1.	6	center*	3½"	triangle
2.	12	medium	3¼"	gem shapes
3.	18	stripped	3½"	triangle
4.	6	light	3½"	triangle

PIECING DIAGRAM
Press seams away from center
Pinch and pin center

WEAVE

1. Cut for one block:

1.	6	center*	3½"	triangle
2.	12	medium	3½"	triangle
3.	48	dark	2⅛"	triangle
4.	12	light	1⅞"	diamond
5.	6	medium	3¼"	diamond

All cutting is based on the 3½" triangle size.

Pieced Strip A

Pieced Strip B And Reverse

Press this seam up or down alternately

← Repeat Fabric*

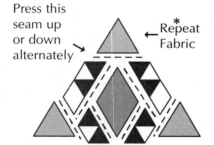

Wedge Piecing Diagram

One Wedge

WEAVE BLOCK

3½" TRIANGLE CENTER REPEAT* FABRIC

Directions:

2. Sew a dark and light 2⅛" strip right sides together with a quarter inch seam down both sides. Cut triangles from the set of strips. Open and press to the dark. Add one dark 2⅛" triangle to make Pieced Strip A as shown. Make 48 of these for one block. Take six and add a light 1⅞" diamond to make Pieced strip B. Take six and make Pieced Strip B Reversed.

3. Assemble a wedge as shown. Make six. Sew the wedges three and three and sew across the middle to make a hexagon block.

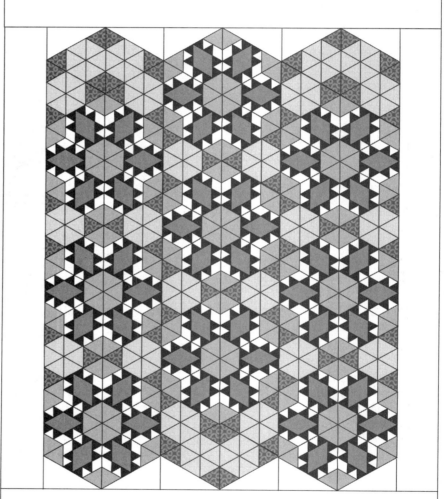

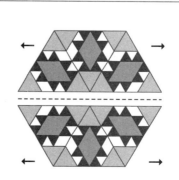

PIECING DIAGRAM
Press seams away from center
Pinch and pin center

DARK EYES

Directions:

2. Sew a dark and light 2⅛" strip right sides together with a quarter inch seam down both sides. Cut triangles from the set of strips. Open and press to the dark. Use two matching triangles plus one dark 2⅛" triangle to make a Pieced Strip. Make 12 of these for one block. Sew onto a medium 3½" triangle as shown.

3. Assemble a wedge as shown below. Make six. Sew the wedges three and three and sew across the middle to make a hexagon block.

All cutting is based on the 3½" triangle size.

1. Cut for one block:

1.	6	center*	3½"	triangle
2.	6	dark	3¼"	diamond
3.	12	medium	3½"	triangle
4.	12	dark	2⅛"	triangle
5.	12	light	3½"	flat pyramid from 1⅞" strip

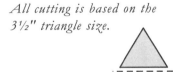

Pieced Strip

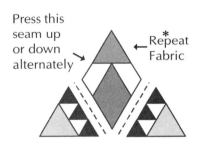

Press this seam up or down alternately

← Repeat Fabric*

Wedge Piecing Diagram

One Wedge

DARK EYES BLOCK

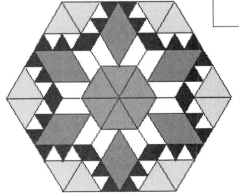

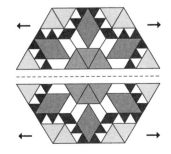

PIECING DIAGRAM
Press seams away from center
Pinch and pin center

37

ARROWHEAD

All cutting is based on the 3½" triangle size.

Directions:

2. Sew a dark and light 2⅛" strip right sides together with a quarter inch seam down both sides. Cut triangles from the set of strips. Open and press to the dark. Add one dark 2⅛" triangle to make a Pieced Strip as shown. Make 12 of these for one block. Sew two 1⅞" light strips and a 3½" medium strip together lengthwise, with the 1⅞" strips on the outside. Cut 4⅞" triangles from both sides of this set of strips.

3. Assemble wedges as shown in diagram at left. Sew wedges three and three and sew across the middle to make a hexagon block.

1. Cut for one block:

1.	6	center*	3½"	triangle
2.	6	medium	3¼"	diamond
3.	12	dark	2⅛"	triangle

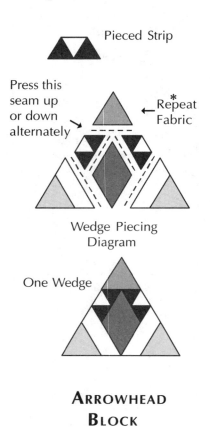

Pieced Strip

Press this seam up or down alternately

Repeat* Fabric

Wedge Piecing Diagram

One Wedge

ARROWHEAD BLOCK

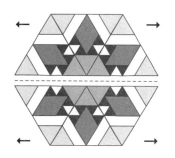

PIECING DIAGRAM
Press seams away from center
Pinch and pin center

MAYFLOWER

Directions:

2. Sew one light 1⅞" diamond and two medium 2⅛" triangles into a pieced triangle A as shown. Make two of these. Use dark triangles and make two B. Assemble with the 3½" triangles in pieced strips as shown to make one wedge. Make six of these.

3. Sew the wedges together into two sets of three. Pinch and pin and sew all the way across to join the two halves and complete the hexagon block.

3½" TRIANGLE CENTER REPEAT* FABRIC

All cutting is based on the 3½" triangle size.

1. Cut for one block:

1.	6	center*, light	3½"	triangle
2.	12	medium	3½"	triangle
3.	24	dark, medium	2⅛"	triangle
4.	24	light	1⅞"	diamond

Pieced Triangles

A.   B.

*
← Repeat
Fabric

Wedge Piecing Diagram

One Wedge

MAYFLOWER BLOCK

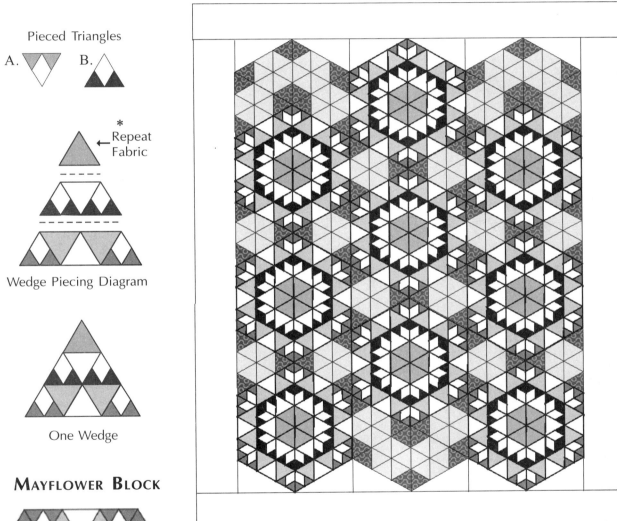

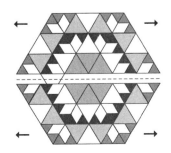

PIECING DIAGRAM
Press seams away
from center
Pinch and pin center

PERIDOT

Directions:

2. Sew a dark and light 1⅞" strip together lengthwise. Make two of these. Press to the dark. Place right sides together, butting seams. Trim to a 60° angle as shown, and cut 1⅞" sections from the strip sets. Sew two sections together as shown to make a pieced diamond. Assemble as shown to make one wedge. Make six.

3. Sew the wedges together into two sets of three. Pinch and pin and sew all the way across to join the two halves and complete the hexagon block.

1. Cut for one block:

1.	6 center*, 6 dark	3½"	triangle
2.	18 medium	3½"	triangle

Strip Set

Assemble Pieced Diamonds

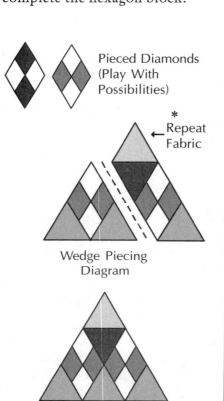

Pieced Diamonds (Play With Possibilities)

Repeat Fabric

Wedge Piecing Diagram

One Wedge

PERIDOT BLOCK

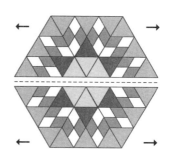

PIECING DIAGRAM
Press seams away from center
Pinch and pin center

Morning Star

Directions:

2. Sew a dark and light 1⅞" strip together lengthwise. Make two of these. Press to the dark. Place right sides together, butting seams. Trim to a 60° angle as shown, and cut 1⅞" sections from the strip sets. Sew two sections together as shown to make a pieced diamond.

3. Make stripped triangles: sew a dark and light 2⅛" strip together lengthwise. Cut 3¾" triangles from the strip. Trim ¼" strip from the bottom of each triangle.

4. Assemble as shown to make one wedge. Make six. Sew the wedges together into two sets of three. Pinch and pin and sew all the way across to join the two halves and complete the hexagon block.

3½" TRIANGLE CENTER REPEAT* FABRIC
All cutting is based on the 3½" triangle size.

1. Cut for one block:

1.	6 center*	3½"	triangle
2.	6 dark	3½"	triangle

Strip Set

Pieced Diamond

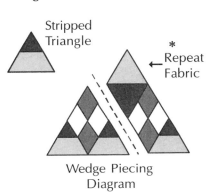

Stripped Triangle

← Repeat Fabric *

Wedge Piecing Diagram

One Wedge

MORNING STAR BLOCK

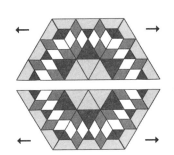

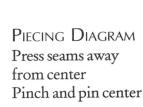

PIECING DIAGRAM
Press seams away from center
Pinch and pin center

SCINTILLATE

All cutting is based on the 3½" triangle size.

1. Cut for one block:

1.	6	center*	3¼"	diamond
2.	6	dark	3½"	triangle
3.	12	light	2⅛"	triangle
4.	12	dark	1⅞"	diamond
5.	12	medium	4⅞"	triangle

Directions:

2. Assemble six wedges as shown in the diagram at left. Sew the wedges three and three and sew across the middle to make a hexagon block.

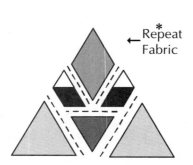

← *Repeat Fabric

Wedge Piecing Diagram

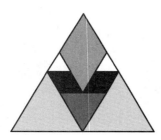

One Wedge

SCINTILLATE BLOCK

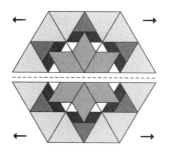

PIECING DIAGRAM
Press seams away from center
Pinch and pin center

Comet

Directions:

2. Sew one dark 1⅞" diamond and two medium 2⅛" triangles into a pieced triangle as shown. Make four of these. Assemble as shown to make one wedge. Make six wedges.

3. Sew the wedges together into two sets of three. Pinch and pin and sew all the way across to join the two halves and complete the hexagon block.

Pieced Triangle

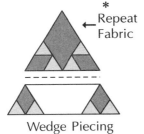
* Repeat Fabric
Wedge Piecing Diagram

One Wedge

Comet Block

3¼" DIAMOND CENTER REPEAT* FABRIC

All cutting is based on the 3½" triangle size.

1. Cut for one block:

1.	6 center*	3¼"	diamond
2.	6 light (3¼" strip)	6¼"	flat pyramid
3.	48 medium	2⅛"	triangle
4.	24 dark	1⅞"	diamond

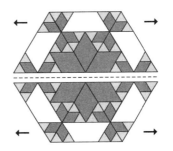

Piecing Diagram
Press seams away from center
Pinch and pin center

43

MARINER'S STAR

Directions:

2. Assemble center diamond, two dark triangles, and a flat pyramid to complete one wedge. Make six.

3. Sew the wedges together into two sets of three. Pinch and pin and sew all the way across to join the two halves and complete the hexagon block.

1. Cut for one block:

1.	6	center*	3¼"	diamond
2.	6	dark	3½"	triangle
3.	6	medium	9"	flat pyramid from 3¼" strip

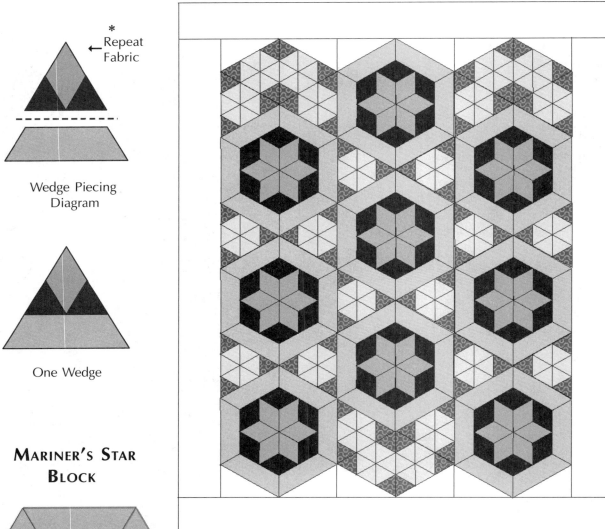

*
← Repeat Fabric

Wedge Piecing Diagram

One Wedge

MARINER'S STAR BLOCK

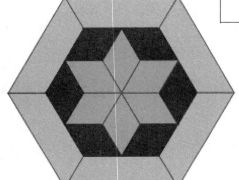

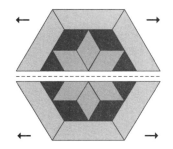

PIECING DIAGRAM
Press seams away from center
Pinch and pin center

GARNET

All cutting is based on the 3½" triangle size.

Directions:

2. Sew a dark and light 1⅞" strip together lengthwise. Make two of these. Press one to the dark and one to the light. Place right sides together, butting seams. Trim to a 60° angle as shown, and cut 1⅞" sections from the strip sets (A). Sew 2⅛" light and medium strips right sides together with a ¼" seam down both sides (sandwich piecing). Cut triangle pairs from this set of strips (B).

3. Assemble pieced strip as shown from a diamond section (A) and a triangle pair (B). Sew the dark triangle to the flat pyramid to make pieced triangles. Assemble as shown to to make one wedge. Make six.

4. Sew the wedges together into two sets of three. Pinch and pin and sew all the way across to join the two halves and complete the hexagon block.

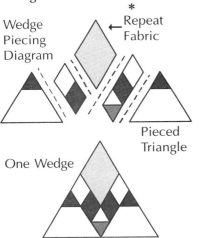

Wedge Piecing Diagram

* Repeat Fabric

Pieced Triangle

One Wedge

GARNET BLOCK

3¼" DIAMOND CENTER REPEAT* FABRIC

1. Cut for one block:

1.	6 center*	3¼"	diamond
2.	6 medium, 6 light, 12 dark	2⅛"	triangle
3.	12 light	4⅞"	flat pyramid from 3¼" strip

 A.

 B. Pieced Strip

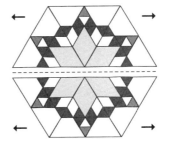

PIECING DIAGRAM
Press seams away from center
Pinch and pin center

DEMURE

All cutting is based on the 3½" triangle size.

Directions:

2. (A) Sew a dark and light 1⅞" strip together lengthwise. Press to the dark. Trim to a 60° angle as shown, and cut 1⅞" sections from the set of strips. (B) Sew a dark 3¼" and light 1⅞" strip together lengthwise. Press to the dark. Trim to a 60° angle as shown, and cut 1⅞" sections from the set of strips (check angle often).

3. Sew one dark 3½" strip and two light 1⅞" strips together lengthwise as shown. Press to the dark. Cut 4⅞" triangles alternately from each side of the set of strips. There will be some waste.

4. Assemble a center diamond, one(A), one(B), and two stripped triangles to complete one wedge. Make six wedges.

5. Sew the wedges together into two sets of three. Pinch and pin and sew all the way across to join the two halves and complete the hexagon block.

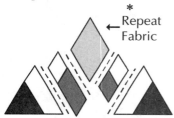

* → Repeat Fabric

Wedge Piecing Diagram

One Wedge

DEMURE BLOCK

3¼" DIAMOND CENTER REPEAT* FABRIC

1. Cut for one block:

1.	6	center*	3¼"	diamond

A.

B.

Stripped Triangles

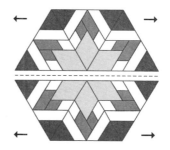

PIECING DIAGRAM
Press seams away
from center
Pinch and pin center

Flag

All cutting is based on the 3½" triangle size.

Directions:

2. Sew a light long diamond and a medium triangle into a pieced flat pyramid as shown. Do the same with a reverse long diamond. Sew with the medium 3½" triangle to make a pieced strip. Sew the center diamond and two dark triangles together and sew onto the pieced strip to make one wedge. Make six of these.

3. Sew the wedges together into two sets of three. Pinch and pin and sew all the way across to join the two halves and complete the hexagon block.

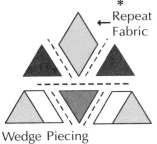

Wedge Piecing Diagram

One Wedge

FLAG BLOCK

3¼" DIAMOND CENTER REPEAT* FABRIC

1. Cut for one block:

1.	6 center*	3¼"	diamond
2.	6 medium, 12 light	3½"	triangle
3.	12 dark	3½"	triangle
4.	6 light, 6 light reverse	3¼"	long diamond cut from a 1⅞" strip

  Pieced Flat Pyramids

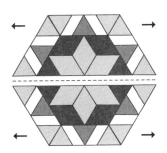

PIECING DIAGRAM

Press seams away from center

Pinch and pin center

PRINCESS

All cutting is based on the 3½" triangle size.

Directions:

2. Sew one dark and one light 2⅛" strip together lengthwise. Cut 3½" triangles from this set of strips. Cut ¼" from the bottom of each pieced triangle. You will get both light and dark-tipped stripped triangles. Use 12 of one kind in each block.

3. Sew one dark and one light 2⅛" strip right sides together with a ¼" seam down both sides. Cut 2⅛" triangles from this set of strips. Pull apart at the tip and press open (matching triangles). You will need 12 for one block. Add a 1⅞" dark or light diamond as shown to the matching triangle set to make a pieced strip and its reverse, or a reversed value strip and its reverse.

4. Assemble as shown to complete one wedge. (Or make with reversed values.) Make six. Sew the wedges together into two sets of three. Pinch and pin and sew across to complete the hexagon block.

Pieced Strips | Reversed Value Pieced Strips

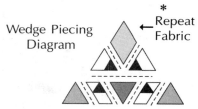

Wedge Piecing Diagram | ← *Repeat Fabric

One Wedge

PRINCESS BLOCK

3¼" DIAMOND CENTER REPEAT* FABRIC

1. Cut for one block:

1.	6	center*	3¼"	diamond
2.	12	medium	3½"	triangle
3.	12	light	1⅞"	diamond
4.	6	dark	3½"	triangle

Light or Dark-tipped Stripped Triangles

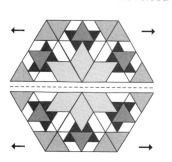

Block With Reversed Values

PIECING DIAGRAM

Press seams away from center
Pinch and pin center

48

Diamonds In Bloom, 69" x 75". A striped fabric to stack produces lots of concentric hexagons, design upon design. Joan used plain 9" triangles for the setting triangles, and added lots of float space around the group of seven DIAMOND blocks. This makes room for a garden of appliqued folk art roses (no pattern given). The strict geometric lines of the blocks contrasts nicely with the organic curves and swirly motion of the rich appliqué. She completes her quilt with a lively SCALLOP border. Now the whole quilt looks like it is in bloom. Pieced and hand quilted by Joan Dawson.

My Violet Garden, 58" x 65". A pieced setting triangle adds dewy sparkle to a classically simple quilt featuring the DAISY block. Bonnie invented this half-block layout which makes fancy corners and edges. I like it so much I used it in my **Tattler** quilt, and showed various ways to use it in the quilt layouts. Pieced and machine quilted by Bonnie Chambers

Coral Rose, (above) 56¼" x 72¾". Two different stacked repeat fabrics add richness of detail to this design. The prints evoke Victorian femininity with soft stripes and polka dots mixing with the roses. A scrappy approach that changes the color accent in the FLAG block and experiments with directional fabric emphasises various points of interest, causing the eye to travel over the quilt. All fabric from the Manor House II collection, Andover Fabrics. Pieced by the author and machine quilted by Judy Irish.

Christmas Cactus, (right) 40" x 52½". A good color rule for quilters is, "All reds go together," which certainly applies to this quilt. Pam chose to use a setting triangle pieced from three red diamonds and three light triangles. This completes the star points for each DARK EYES block. A very rich design, it makes a quilt larger than you'd expect from only four blocks. Pieced and machine quilted by Pam Cope.

Butterflies In The Willows, 67" x 75". The WEAVE block gives this quilt a feathered star look, with lots of little triangles. Joan used the harder layout for this quilt from pg. 111, which requires careful planning and construction of each part of the quilt. Lay it all out on a quilt wall before beginning to sew it together. Appliqued detail in the corners and a pieced border add to the richness of the whole design. So far, awards given this quilt include a First Place in the professional division and Reserve Grand Champion, also in the professional division, at the Puyallup Fair, a very large state fair in Washington near Seattle. Pieced by Joan Dawson and machine quilted by Judy Irish.

Floral Flamenco, 71½" x 89". This quilt is pieced entirely from prints in the Pat L. Nickols Collection III by P&B Textiles, based on antique fabrics from 1840 or earlier. The author wanted to emphasize the diamond shape that was showing up around the edges of the two blocks, MARS and SUNSET, so she struggled on graph paper until she put together the design for the CHAIN LINK border. This frothy finish is perfect to frame the details of the busy pastel and floral prints in the body of the quilt. Machine quilted by Judy Irish.

Butterflies For Paris, (above) 68" x 72". The bright colors and whirling motifs in this quilt evoke images of ferris wheels and other rides at the state fair, with fireworks overhead. Lots of excitement, lots of fun. It's interesting to compare this version of the MORNING block with the quilt on pg. 59 by Kathy Kryla. Each block design presents many possibilities. Pieced by Kathleen Springer and machine quilted by Marianne Roan.

Garnet, (above right) 65¾" x 82½". Kathie's choices of light warm bright fabrics are an incandescent glow against the background of medium green. A pieced border that looks like ground cover adds a garden touch to these glorious blossoms. The GARNET block is named after a gemstone, but at least these softer flowers will last a long time in fabric. Pieced by Kathie Kryla and machine quilted by Judy Irish.

Cherry Pie, (right) 57" x 77½", started with a fabric the author bid for on eBay, eventually paying more than $30 a yard. Red cherries and green stems and leaves stack up for beautiful designs in the ARROWHEAD block. Then Judy Irish contributed a rose fabric that is the beautiful toasty beige color of a perfect pie crust. (With a little sugar sprinkled on, can't help it, it makes me think of food.) The whole thing is framed in a reddish-pink busy print like pie filling. Machine quilted by Judy Irish.

53

Partridge In A Pear Tree (above left), 58" x 62", and **Emmanuel Starlight** (above right), 60" x 62", are just two of the quilts Linda has made so far using the Combination Layout on pg. 99. She chose MORNING LIGHT for the central 3-Row block, and NATIVE for the surrounding six 2-Row blocks. She began to make a few Christmas quilts for gifts, then her Dad gave his to a freind, so she had to make him another, then one for herself, etc. Last I heard, she had made ten of these altogether. Each one is gorgeous. I chose to show you three. (See Star of Wonder, pg. 57.) Pieced by Linda DeGaeta and quilted by Janice Hairston.

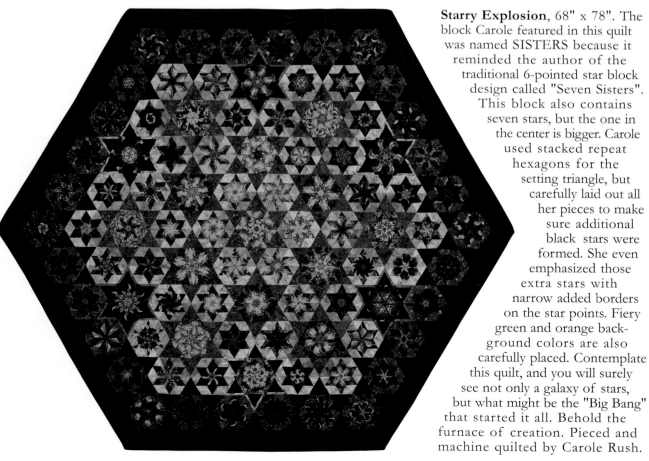

Starry Explosion, 68" x 78". The block Carole featured in this quilt was named SISTERS because it reminded the author of the traditional 6-pointed star block design called "Seven Sisters". This block also contains seven stars, but the one in the center is bigger. Carole used stacked repeat hexagons for the setting triangle, but carefully laid out all her pieces to make sure additional black stars were formed. She even emphasized those extra stars with narrow added borders on the star points. Fiery green and orange background colors are also carefully placed. Contemplate this quilt, and you will surely see not only a galaxy of stars, but what might be the "Big Bang" that started it all. Behold the furnace of creation. Pieced and machine quilted by Carole Rush.

Royal, 70" x 88". Stylized cats on a black background stack up to become strange curled or whirling petals in a midnight garden. The rich neon color gradations in RaNae Merrill's Radiant Collection of brush-stroked almost solids adds extra punch and glow. The block name, PRINCESS, inspired the name for the CROWN border and the quilt name. Judy Irish added to the unique look of this quilt with machine quilted fluffy dragonflies (the quilt cats love them), suns, and more. What a flight of imagination! All fabric from Blank Textiles.

Cancun Neon, 70½" x 78¾". The author once wanted to be an icthyologist (a biologist that studies fish), probably because fish are so beautiful. Now this quilt was fun! A fabric showing realistic-looking fish was the inspiration for a sampler quilt of 2-Row blocks. The variety of blocks used emphasises the beauty and complexity of the undersea world with diatoms, fish, and other undersea creatures. Can you see the transclucent fish with a lot of personality that the machine quilter added throughout? Blocks used are: CHEVRON, CRYSTAL, DOG-WOOD, MOSS AGATE, NATIVE, OPAL, SIMPLE STAR, SUN, THISTLE, TINY HEX, TINY STAR, TINY PINWHEEL, AND WINDOW. The SURF border adds a bit of froth around the edge. Pieced by the author and machine quilted by Judy Irish.

56

Star Of Wonder (above), 60" x 60", is another in the series of Christmas quilts (see pg. 54) made by Linda DeGaeta. Linda is not afraid to try different recipes for fabric placement in her blocks. In this quilt, shades of blue work well with ornate gold fabrics. Machine quilted by Janice Hairston.

Midnight Sunflower (above), 79" x 100". Kate knows all about the midnight sun, since she lives in Bethel, Alaska. Unusual fabric choices add soft detail to this strong arrangement. Kate put four GLASS blocks into the triangle halves that square off seven BEADING blocks. She also completed the sunny yellow hexes along the edges of the central bouquet to create a more ornate design. Pieced by Kate McIntyre and machine quilted by Allison Broerman.

Moonlight Becomes You (left), 66" x 80". Light and dark blues, pale pink, and lavender combine to create a magic wash of moonlight and faerie stars. Some of the fabric has an iridescent or sparkling coating which adds to the misty mood. As well, the geometry of the PYRITE block and lots of stars in the setting triangles add to the drifting spell of this dreamy fabric combination. Pieced by Linda DeGaeta and machine quilted by Janice Hairston.

Hidden Star (above), 68" x 76½". Earthy color choices create a sophisticated design with plenty of quiet details to enjoy. The combination is reminiscent of forest leaves and the soft light of the understory. Six outside PERIDOT blocks softly turn around the central "hidden star". Pieced by Kathy Lee and machine quilted by Lynn Reppas.

Gardens Of Paris (above right), 64" x 82", again demonstrates how the quilter's choice of high contrast prints brings out little details to create endless designs repeating themselves across the surface of the quilt. Placement of the light fabric within each DEMURE block reveals a garden of wide-open flower faces reaching for the sun. Pieced by Kathleen Malarky and machine quilted by Judy Irish.

Flamingos In Paradise (left), 74" x 79". Light pink and blue on black makes striking designs in these JADE blocks. Linda used stacked repeats both in the center gem shapes and also in the flat pyramids that echo the center shape. The graded blue background looks like light playing within a pool of clear, clean water. Have a vacation just looking at this quilt! Half-blocks in the four corners complete this design. Pieced by Linda DeGaeta and machine quilted by Janice Hairston.

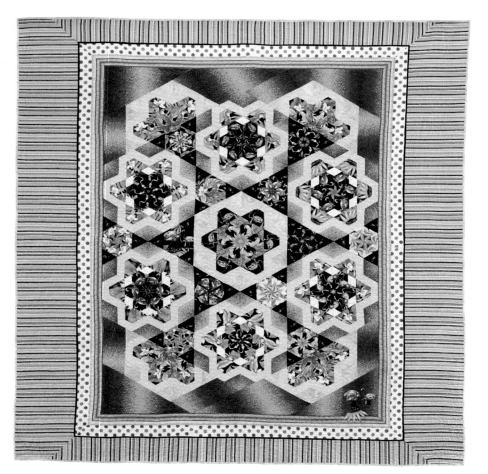

Morning Light, 68" x 79½". Kathie used the MORNING block to create a light-saturated piece of softly manipulated fabric that will be a quiet pleasure to live with. Compare it to Kathleen Springer's quilt on pg. 53, which uses the same block, but is spinning with action and fun. Both beautiful. Here a thin line holds the center hexagon and is echoed in the narrow stems of the folk appliqué. Stronger, but still narrow, the two outside plain navy borders enclose the pieced PEEKABOO border which softly echoes the stacked repeats in the quilt. Did you notice that the petals of the appliqué flowers are also stacked repeats? Work it, work it girl! Pieced by Kathie Kryla and machine quilted by Dawn Kelley.

Black & White With A Little Red (above left), 31" x 22". This color combination always looks good. Janet gets really strong repeat designs in the SPINNER block from this high contrast print and adding more red puts in extra punch. Plenty to look at for such a little quilt! Pieced and machine quilted by Janet Goad.

Asian Jewels (above right), 51" x 54", uses Janet's beautiful new layout for 2-Row blocks. AMBER looks like heirloom embroidery with a delicate printed pattern in each narrow outside strip. This same fabric stripe was used to wonderful effect in the final border of the quilt. A great example of letting the fabric tell you what to do! Also notice the small half-hexes in the four corners of the STRING OF PEARLS border. Pieced by Janet Goad and machine quilted by Linda Daughetee.

Stargazing (left), 72" x 80". Linda chose an ornate striped fabric and the result is stars and medallions with a feeling of antiquity. The narrow block border also frames the setting triangles creating a lattice-work effect. The MORNING STAR block here looks like cathedral windows. She's not afraid to play with a mix of setting triangles - some stacked and some stars and some diamonds and triangles. It's abstract art! Pieced by Linda DeGaeta and machine quilted by Janice Hairston.

Winter Garden, 65" x 79", was inspired by a piece of polished cotton obtained on eBay, featuring large lilacs and camellias on black. Purple, gray and blue in the TAMBOURINE block creates starry snowflakes falling onto frosty flowers and branches. There are flowers for every month of the year. Maybe, though, the machine quilter didn't know the name of this quilt when she added a hummingbird doing back flips. Hummingbirds mostly spend the winter in South America. The DIAMOND LACE border was the author's first pieced border for these quilts. The quilt called for it! Machine quilted by Judy Irish.

Thirties Sampler, 66" x 83", is assembled from thirties prints obtained at garage sales, eBay, and antique stores in Iowa the author visited while on a teaching trip. Scraps were used as well as yards of fabric. Blocks used in this quilt are: MAYFLOWER, MILL WHEEL, COMET, JESTER, TOPAZ, JEWEL, FROST, and TINY PINWHEEL. 2-Row blocks were made larger with a plain outside frame. Setting triangles are stacked hexes or hollow hexes, and a couple of pinwheels. The ICE CREAM border is true to the thirties theme. Machine quilted by Judy Irish.

The Avian Winter Ball, 70" x 70", combines strong colors and lots of stars for a happy, lively, party atmosphere. Pam took the star points from the MOTHER OF PEARL block and multiplied them in the TIPI border. Choosing a part of the block often is a great way to create a border design. Pam added stripped green-tipped triangles as background in the border (also part of the block). Pieced and machine quilted by Pam Pifer.

Folk Hearts, 66" x 70". Virginia is very good at combining many busy prints to get lots of texture and pattern. The FOLK HEARTS blocks are surrounded by stacked repeat setting triangles that, thanks to the fabric, look like light-hearted decorative tole paintings. The color choices in this quilt are sophisticated, rich and satisfying. Pieced by Virginia Anderson.

The three quilts on this page are part of a Serendipity round robin. Each person chose her repeat fabric, and pieced 4⅞" hexagons for the centers of the blocks. **Icons** (above left), 64½" x 78", was started by the author. Joan Hanson finished the VENUS blocks, and Pam Cope devised clever setting triangles. After I put it all together, I added a STRING OF PEARLS border. Machine quilted by Judy Irish.

Fiesta Ware (above right), 52" x 66½". Pam Cope chose a light happy print that looks like a thirties tablecloth. I added more pastels to complete the SWAN blocks, and Joan Hanson completed the Three Diamond setting triangles. Machine quilted by Pam Cope.

Thomas & Lori's Quilt (left), 61" x 86". Joan made the block centers from a Japanese-themed fabric. Pam completed the SWAN blocks, and I made the Three Diamond setting triangles. Note the smaller stars in the four corners of the quilt. It's interesting that similar choices were made by the round robin participants. Two used the same blocks, two used the same border. Many more possibilities exist.

Tambourine

Directions:

2. Sew two dark 2⅛" triangles onto one light 1⅞" diamond to make a pieced triangle as shown. Make two of these. Sew two flat pyramids and a 3½" triangle into a pieced strip.

3. Assemble as shown to make one wedge. Make six. Sew the wedges together into two sets of three. Pinch and pin and sew all the way across to join the two halves and complete the hexagon block.

Pieced Triangle

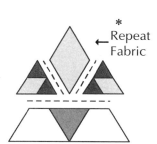

← Repeat Fabric

Wedge Piecing Diagram

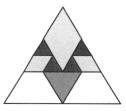

One Wedge

TAMBOURINE BLOCK

3¼" DIAMOND CENTER REPEAT* FABRIC

All cutting is based on the 3½" triangle size.

1. Cut for one block:

1.	6	center*	3¼"	diamond
2.	24	dark	2⅛"	triangle
3.	12	light	1⅞"	diamond
4.	6	medium	3½"	triangle
5.	12	light	4⅞"	flat pyramid from 3½" strip

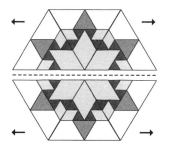

PIECING DIAGRAM
Press seams away from center
Pinch and pin center

65

MORNING

Directions:
2. Sew a dark and light 1⅞" strip together lengthwise. Make two of these. Press to the dark. Place right sides together, butting seams. Trim to a 60° angle as shown, and cut 1⅞" sections from the strip sets. Sew two sections together as shown to make a pieced diamond. Assemble as shown to make one wedge. Make six.

3. Sew the wedges together into two sets of three. Pinch and pin and sew all the way across to join the two halves and complete the hexagon block.

3¼" DIAMOND CENTER REPEAT* FABRIC
All cutting is based on the 3½" triangle size.

1. Cut for one block:

1.	6 center*	3¼"	diamond
2.	12 medium, 6 light	3½"	triangle

Strip Set

Pieced Diamond

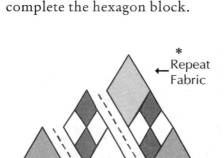

← * Repeat Fabric

Wedge Piecing Diagram

One Wedge

MORNING BLOCK

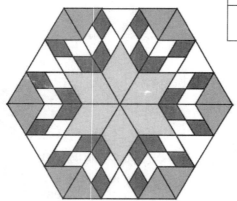

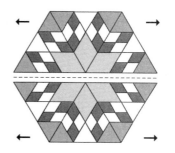

PIECING DIAGRAM
Press seams away from center
Pinch and pin center

66

AGATE

Directions:

2. Sew a dark and light 1⅞" strip together lengthwise. Make two of these. Press to the dark. Place right sides together, dark to dark and light to light. Trim to a 60° angle as shown, and cut 3¼" sections from the sets of strips. Assemble all as shown to make one wedge. Make six.

3. Sew the wedges together into two sets of three. Pinch and pin and sew all the way across to join the two halves and complete the hexagon block.

1. Cut for one block:

1.	6 center*	3¼"	diamond
2.	12 light, 6 medium	3½"	triangle

Strip Set

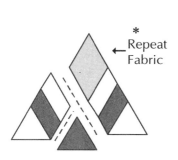

← * Repeat Fabric

Wedge Piecing Diagram

One Wedge

AGATE BLOCK

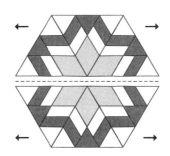

PIECING DIAGRAM
Press seams away from center
Pinch and pin center

TOPAZ

Directions:

2. Cut a 1⅝" triangle from one end of the center* diamond. Then sew a dark 2⅛" triangle on that end to make a Pieced Diamond A.

3. Sew a dark and light 1⅞" strip together lengthwise. Press to the dark. (If making more than one block, make two of these. Place right sides together, butting seams.) Trim to a 60° angle as shown, and cut 1⅞" sections from the strip sets. Sew two sections together as shown to make a Pieced Diamond B. Make 12 for each block.

4. Assemble as shown to make one wedge. Make six. Sew the wedges together into two sets of three. Pinch and pin and sew all the way across to join the two halves and complete the hexagon block.

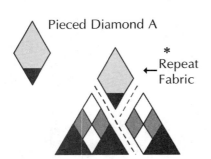

Pieced Diamond A

*
← Repeat Fabric

Wedge Piecing Diagram

One Wedge

TOPAZ BLOCK

3¼" DIAMOND CENTER REPEAT* FABRIC

All cutting is based on the 3½" triangle size.

1. Cut for one block:

1.	6 center*	3¼"	diamond
2.	6 dark	3½"	triangle
3.	6 dark	2⅛"	triangle

Strip Set

Pieced Diamond B

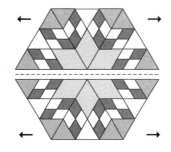

PIECING DIAGRAM
Press seams away from center
Pinch and pin center

ONYX

Directions:

2. Cut a 1⅝" triangle from one end of all the center* diamonds. (Cut while still stacked.) Then sew a dark 2⅛" triangle on that end to make a dark-tipped diamond.

3. Sew a dark and light 1⅞" strip together lengthwise. Make two of these. Press to the dark. Place right sides together, dark to dark and light to light. Trim to a 60° angle as shown, and cut 1⅞" sections from the sets of strips. Assemble all as shown to make one wedge. Make six.

4. Sew the wedges together into two sets of three. Pinch and pin and sew all the way across to complete the hexagon block.

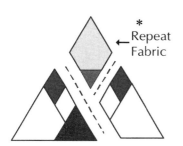

Wedge Piecing
Diagram

One Wedge

ONYX BLOCK

3¼" DIAMOND CENTER REPEAT* FABRIC

All cutting is based on the 3½" triangle size.

1. Cut for one block:

1.	6 center*	3¼"	diamond
2.	6 dark	3½"	triangle
3.	6 dark	2⅛"	triangle
4.	12 light	4⅞"	flat pyramid from a 3¼" strip

Strip Set

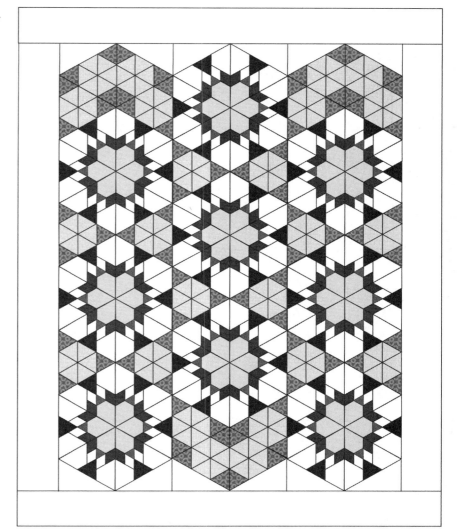

PIECING DIAGRAM
Press seams away
from center
Pinch and pin center

Mother Of Pearl

Directions:

2. Sew a light and a dark 2⅛" strip together lengthwise. Cut 3¾" triangles from this strip set. Trim ¼" off the bottom. (Stripped Triangle A) Sew a 2¾" medium strip and a 2⅝" light strip together lengthwise. Cut 4⅞" triangles from this strip set. (Stripped Triangle B) Cut a 1⅝" triangle from one end of the center* diamond. Sew a dark 2⅛" triangle onto two seperate corners of the trimmed center diamond to make a pieced triangle.

3. Assemble as shown to make one wedge. Make six. Sew the wedges three and three and sew across the middle to complete the hexagon block.

Wedge Piecing Diagram

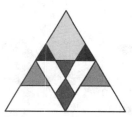

One Wedge

MOTHER OF PEARL BLOCK

3¼" DIAMOND CENTER REPEAT* FABRIC

1. Cut for one block:

1.	6	center*	3¼"	diamond
2.	6	dark	2⅛"	triangle
3.	6	dark	1⅞"	dia mond
4.	6	light	3½"	flat pyramid from 1⅞" strip

Stripped Triangle A

Stripped Triangle B

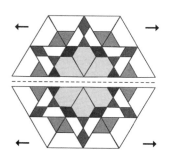

All cutting is based on the 3½" triangle size.

PIECING DIAGRAM

Press seams away from center

Pinch and pin center

PYRITE

Directions:

2. Sew a light and a dark 2⅛" strip together lengthwise. Cut 3¾" triangles from this strip set. Trim ¼" off the bottom. (Stripped Triangle) Cut a 1⅝" triangle from one end of all the center* diamonds. (Cut while still stacked.) Then sew a dark 2⅛" triangle on that end to make a dark-tipped pieced diamond.

3. Assemble as shown to make one wedge. Make six. Sew the wedges three and three and sew across the middle to complete the hexagon block.

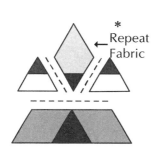

Wedge Piecing Diagram

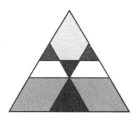

One Wedge

PYRITE BLOCK

1. Cut for one block:

1.	6	center*	3¼"	diamond
2.	6	dark	2⅛"	triangle
3.	6	med	3¼"	diamond
4.	6	dark	3½"	triangle

Stripped Triangle

Pieced Diamond

All cutting is based on the 3½" triangle size.

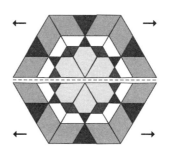

PIECING DIAGRAM

Press seams away from center

Pinch and pin center

71

JADE

Directions:

2. Cut a 1⅝" triangle from one end of the center* diamond. Sew a dark 2⅛" triangle onto two seperate corners of the trimmed center diamond to make a pieced triangle. Assemble the cut pieces as shown to make one wedge. Make six of these.

3. Sew the wedges three and three and sew across the middle to complete the hexagon block.

1. Cut for one block:

1.	6	center*	3¼"	diamond
2.	12	dark	2⅛"	triangle
3.	12	medium	3½"	triangle
4.	6	medium	4⅞"	flat pyr. 3¼" strip
5.	12	light	3½"	flat pyramid from
6.	6	light	4⅞"	1⅞" strip

All cutting is based on the 3½" triangle size.

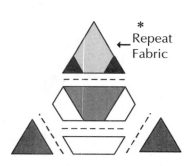

Wedge Piecing Diagram

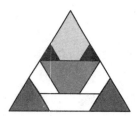

One Wedge

JADE BLOCK

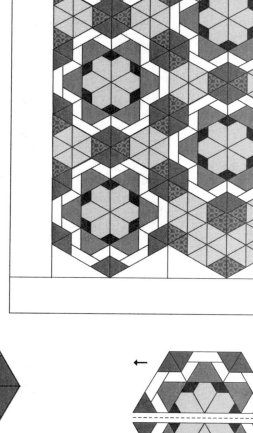

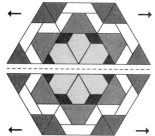

PIECING DIAGRAM
Press seams away
from center
Pinch and pin center

Diamond

All cutting is based on the 3½" triangle size.

1. Cut for one block:

1.	6	center*	4⅞"	triangle
2.	6	light	2⅛"	triangle
3.	6	dark	3½"	triangle
4.	12	dark	3½"	flat pyramid from 1⅞" strip

Directions:

2. Make 12 sets of sandwich-pieced 3½" triangles. Use two sets plus a 3½" dark triangle to make strip (A). Use two flat pyramids plus a 2⅛" triangle to make strip (B). Assemble as shown to make one wedge. Make six of these.

3. Sew the wedges three and three and sew across the middle to complete the hexagon block.

Pieced Strip A

Pieced Strip B

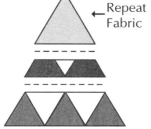

*
← Repeat Fabric

Wedge Piecing Diagram

One Wedge

Diamond Block

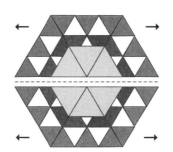

Piecing Diagram
Press seams away from center
Pinch and pin center

MARS

All cutting is based on the 3½" triangle size.

1. Cut for one block:

1.	6	center*	4⅞"	triangle
2.	6	dark	4⅞"	triangle

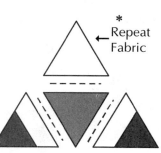

← Repeat Fabric

Wedge Piecing Diagram

One Wedge

MARS BLOCK

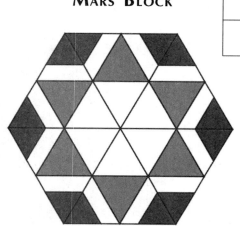

4⅞" TRIANGLE CENTER REPEAT* FABRIC

Directions:

2. Cut a 3½" dark strip and two 1⅞" light strips. Sew together lengthwise, with the narrow light strips on the outside. From this set of strips, cut 4⅞" triangles from both sides. There will be some waste. Assemble with a center* triangle and a dark triangle to make one wedge. Make six of these.

3. Sew the wedges three and three and sew across the middle to complete the hexagon block.

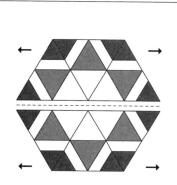

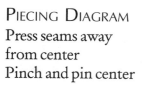

PIECING DIAGRAM

Press seams away from center

Pinch and pin center

SWAN

1. Cut for one block:

1.	6	center*	4⅞"	triangle
2.	6	light	2⅛"	triangle
3.	6	medium	3½"	triangle

Directions:

2. Make 2⅛" (need 18 for one block) and 3½" matching triangles (need 12 for one block) according to the directions on pg. 12. From these make strips (A) and (B) as shown. Assemble with a center* triangle to make one wedge. Make six of these.

3. Sew the wedges three and three and sew across the middle to complete the hexagon block.

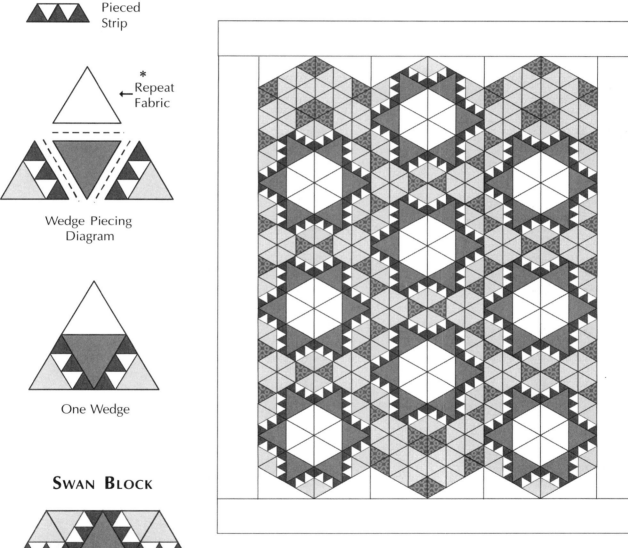

Pieced Strip

← Repeat Fabric

Wedge Piecing Diagram

One Wedge

SWAN BLOCK

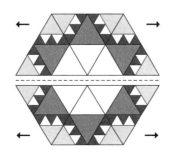

PIECING DIAGRAM
Press seams away from center
Pinch and pin center

75

VENUS

1. Cut for one block:

1.	6	center*	4⅞"	triangle
2.	18	dark	1⅞"	diamond
3.	18	light	2⅛"	triangle

Pieced Unit

Pieced Triangle

Pieced Strip

Stripped Triangle

* Repeat Fabric ←

Wedge Piecing Diagram

One Wedge

VENUS BLOCK

Directions:

2. Sew a light 3½" strip to two 2⅛" medium strips lengthwise, with the medium strips on the outside. From this set of strips, cut 4⅞" stripped triangles from both sides. There will be some waste. From the 1⅞" diamonds and the 2⅛" triangles, make the pieced triangle and the pieced strip. Assemble these together as shown. Combine two stripped triangles, the pieced unit, and a center* triangle to make one wedge. Make six of these.

3. Sew the wedges three and three and sew across the middle to complete the hexagon block.

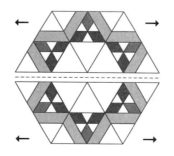

PIECING DIAGRAM
Press seams away from center
Pinch and pin center

Sunset

Directions:

2. Cut two 1¼" strips and one 3⅜" strip and sew together lengthwise with the narrow strips on the outside. Cut 4⅛" triangles from this set of strips. Cut another 1¼" strip and log cabin it onto another side of the 3⅜" light triangle. Press and trim to 4⅞" as necessary. Make six of these.

3. Cut two 2⅛" strips and one 1⅞" strip (different colors)and sew together lengthwise with the wider strips on the outside. Cut 5⅛" triangles from this set of strips. Cut ¼" from the bottom of each triangle. Make 12 the same of these.

4. Assemble the blocks as shown, or if you had premade centers, use the alternate assembly diagram.

Wedge Piecing Diagram

One Wedge

Sunset Block

1. Cut for one block:

1.	6	center*	4⅞"	triangle	
2.	6	light	3½"	triangle	

Log Cabin another strip onto light triangle and trim to 4⅞"

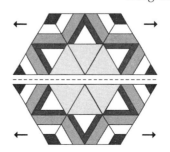

Alternate Assembly Diagram

Piecing Diagram

Press seams away from center

Pinch and pin center

77

RUFFLES

Directions:

2. Sew two small diamonds and a flat pyramid into strip (A). Sew two large diamonds and one light triangle into strip (B). Assemble with a center* triangle to make one wedge. Make six of these.

3. Sew the wedges three and three and sew across the middle to complete the hexagon block.

1. Cut for one block:

1.	6	center*	4⅞"	triangle
2.	6	light	3½"	triangle
3.	12	medium	3¼"	diamond
4.	12	light	1⅞"	diamond
5.	6	medium	3½"	flat pyramid from 1⅞" strip

All cutting is based on the 3½" triangle size.

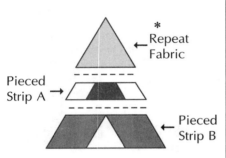

Repeat Fabric *

Pieced Strip A →

← Pieced Strip B

Wedge Piecing Diagram

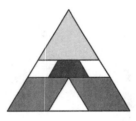

One Wedge

RUFFLES BLOCK

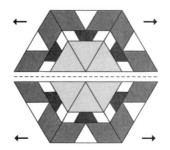

PIECING DIAGRAM
Press seams away from center
Pinch and pin center

78

VISUAL INDEX OF PIECED BORDERS

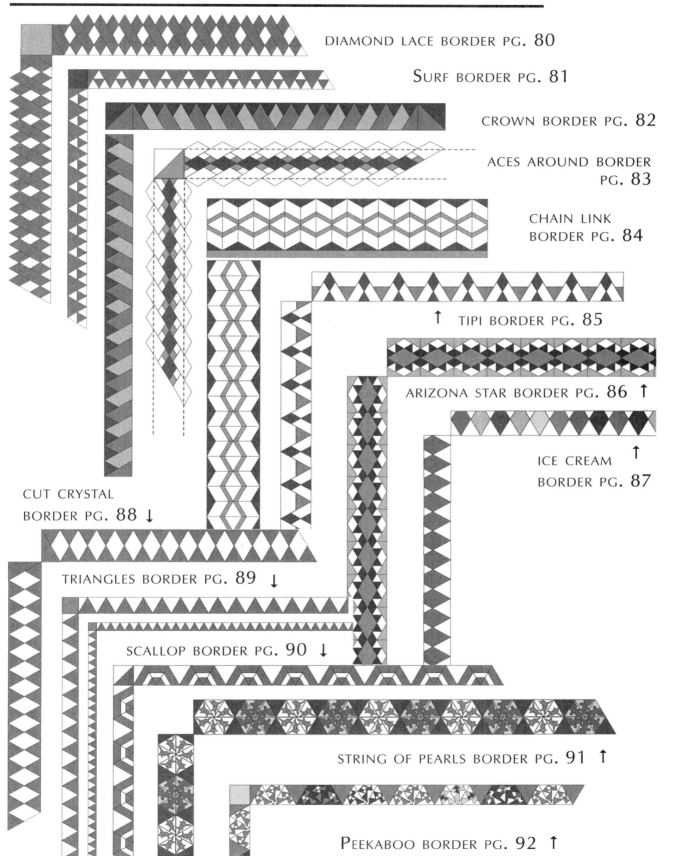

DIAMOND LACE BORDER PG. 80

SURF BORDER PG. 81

CROWN BORDER PG. 82

ACES AROUND BORDER PG. 83

CHAIN LINK BORDER PG. 84

↑ TIPI BORDER PG. 85

ARIZONA STAR BORDER PG. 86 ↑

ICE CREAM BORDER PG. 87 ↑

CUT CRYSTAL BORDER PG. 88 ↓

TRIANGLES BORDER PG. 89 ↓

SCALLOP BORDER PG. 90 ↓

STRING OF PEARLS BORDER PG. 91 ↑

PEEKABOO BORDER PG. 92 ↑

DIAMOND LACE BORDER: TWO PIECED STRIPS MAKE A FANCY BORDER FOR A QUILT.

Trim

CUT AND ASSEMBLE:

1. Strip #1: Cut a 5½" strip of the background and trim to a 60° angle as shown. Then cut 1⅞" sections from this strip. Check the angle often to make sure it stays 60°. Sew a 2⅛" triangle onto this strip as shown. Press to the triangle.

2. Strip #2: Cut three 1⅞" strips of fabric, two of the background color and one of a border color. Sew the three strips together lengthwise with the background color on the outside. Offset the ends to get the most sections out of the strip set. Trim to a 60° angle as shown. Then cut 1⅞" sections from this strip. Check the angle often to make sure it stays 60°. Sew a 2⅛" triangle onto this strip as shown. Press to the triangle. The other two seams should be pressed away from the triangle.

3. Sew the two strips together alternately as shown to create the border. Press along the length of the border. Trim the outside jagged edge to a straight edge with a wide ruler and a rotary cutter. I added a 2" strip of the background color as the final outside border for a little float space, and to make the outside edge stronger. For the WINTER GARDEN quilt, I used 32 strips top and bottom and 44 strips on each of the sides. Add an extra strip #1 as needed to make the design symmetrical. Finish the ends by squaring each end off with a 5" triangle half and use a 4½" corner square added on the left and right of the last two borders you put on.

This is a border with a bit of stretch to it, so it is very forgiving and easy to adjust to the measurement of the quilt. Add or remove strips to make it the right length.

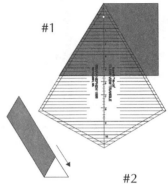

#1

#2

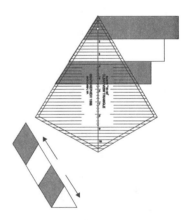

#3

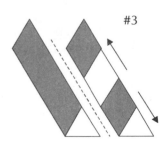

Sew #1 and #2 Together

FINISH LEFT & RIGHT ENDS OF BORDER

Cut Triangle Halves From a 2⅞" x 5" Rectangle

SURF BORDER: A PIECED TRIANGLE ALTERNATING WITH A PLAIN TRIANGLE ADDS SOME SPARKLE AND FROTH AROUND THE OUTSIDE OF YOUR QUILT.

CUT AND ASSEMBLE:

1. **To make the Pieced Triangle:** sandwich-piece 2⅛" matching triangles from a light and a dark 2⅛" strip. To a matching triangle, add two plain 2⅛" (light or dark) triangles to make a Pieced Triangle as shown.

2. Alternate the Pieced Triangle with a plain (light or dark) 3½" triangle. Keep adding these alternately to make the correct length of border. For the CANCUN NEON quilt, first the plain blue inner border is cut 3½" wide. Then the top and bottom SURF borders are 18 pairs of pieced-plain triangles plus one pieced triangle. Left and right SURF borders are 21 pairs plus one pieced triangle.

3. Square off the ends of each pieced border with a left or right triangle half from a 2⅜" x 4" rectangle. After you put on the left and right SURF borders, add a 3¼" square on each end of the top and bottom border. I added a final 2" outer border to stabilize the edges for quilting, and for a little float space, for a finished quilt size of 70½" x 78¾".

This is a border with a bit of stretch to it, so it is another forgiving and easy to adjust design that would suit many 60° quilt patterns. Add or remove a unit to bring it closer to the needed measurement. Of course, you may wish to measure the top before adding inner borders, measure the pieced borders, and then choose a width for the inner border that will make everything fit perfectly.

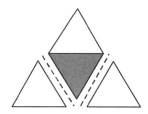

Pieced Triangle

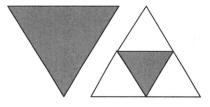

Pieced-Plain Pair

FINISH ENDS OF BORDER SECTIONS
Cut Triangle Halves From a 2⅜" x 4" Rectangle

Triangle Halves

FINISH ENDS OF ROWS

CROWN BORDER: LARGE PIECES MAKE THIS BORDER GO TOGETHER FAST, AND IT LOOKS IMPRESSIVE.

CUT AND ASSEMBLE:

1. **To make the Flat Pyramid Unit:** cut a flat pyramid from a 3¼" strip at 6¼" on the Super 60™. Sew on a 3½" triangle as shown to make the Flat Pyramid Unit or its reverse.

Flat Pyramid
Unit & Reverse

2. **To make a Pieced Center:** Sew two 3½" triangles to a 3¼" diamond as shown. Choose the Pieced Center, OR the Alternate Pieced Center to help fit the border to the quilt top. For the ROYAL quilt, first the black inner border was cut 3¼" wide. Then the top and bottom CROWN borders are eight left and eight right Flat Pyramid Units, with a Pieced Center. Left and right CROWN borders are 10 left and 10 right Flat Pyramid Units with the Alternate Pieced Center.

Pieced Center

COMMANDO BORDERING: The top border was definitely ruffley after I sewed it on. I decided to adjust the fit by taking an extra ⅛" in the seam between each two Flat Pyramid Units. (See the arrows on the diagram.) Then it fit perfectly. When I assembled the bottom border, I sewed each seam between two Flat Pyramid Units at ⅜" instead of ¼". Again, it fit perfectly. Perhaps if the left and right inner borders were wider, the top and bottom borders would not need this adjustment. Would that look good?

Alternate Pieced
Center

3. Square off the ends of each pieced border panel with a left or right triangle half from a 3⅞" x 6¼" rectangle. After you put on the left and right CROWN borders, add a 6" half-square on each end of the top and bottom border. (Cut a 6½" square of each color. Cut both in half diagonally. Sew the two different colored triangles together to make a square divided diagonally into two colors.) I added a final 2" outer border to stabilize the edges for quilting, and for a little float space, for a finished quilt top size of 70" x 88".

Cut Triangle Halves
From a 3⅞" x 6¾"
Rectangle

FINISH
ENDS OF
ROWS

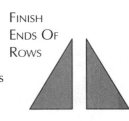

Triangle Halves

This border is not easy to fit to just any size of quilt, partly because it is symmetrical in each panel, so the left and right sides of each panel need to have the same number of units. I followed the grid lines to estimate how many units needed to be in each border panel. At least the two different pieced centers allow for some adjustment in border length. This is a showy design that would flatter many 60° quilt patterns.

Half-Square

ACES AROUND BORDER: WITH A LOOK LIKE WOVEN RIBBON, THIS BORDER FITS MANY BLOCKS.

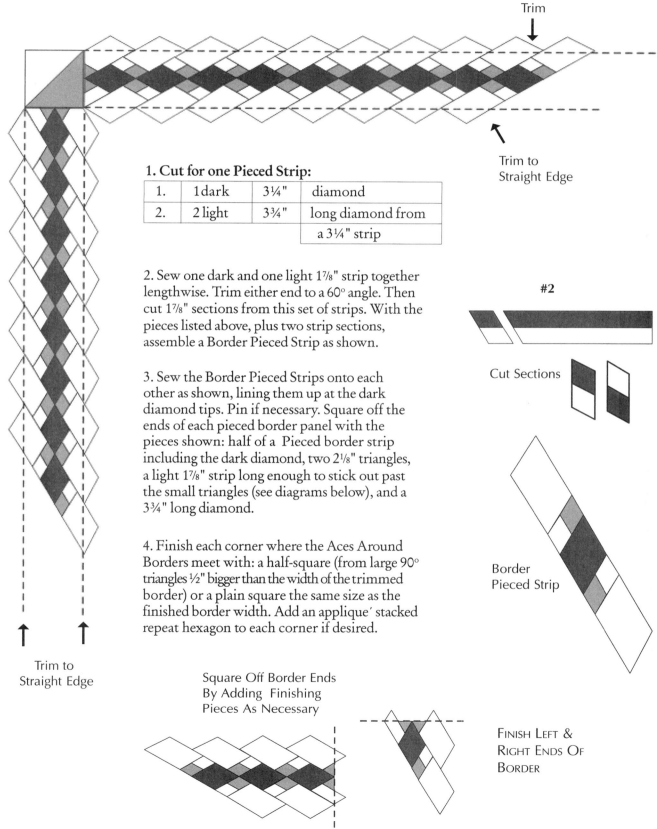

Trim

Trim to
Straight Edge

1. Cut for one Pieced Strip:

1.	1 dark	3¼"	diamond
2.	2 light	3¾"	long diamond from a 3¼" strip

2. Sew one dark and one light 1⅞" strip together lengthwise. Trim either end to a 60° angle. Then cut 1⅞" sections from this set of strips. With the pieces listed above, plus two strip sections, assemble a Border Pieced Strip as shown.

3. Sew the Border Pieced Strips onto each other as shown, lining them up at the dark diamond tips. Pin if necessary. Square off the ends of each pieced border panel with the pieces shown: half of a Pieced border strip including the dark diamond, two 2⅛" triangles, a light 1⅞" strip long enough to stick out past the small triangles (see diagrams below), and a 3¾" long diamond.

4. Finish each corner where the Aces Around Borders meet with: a half-square (from large 90° triangles ½" bigger than the width of the trimmed border) or a plain square the same size as the finished border width. Add an appliqué stacked repeat hexagon to each corner if desired.

#2

Cut Sections

Border
Pieced Strip

Trim to
Straight Edge

Square Off Border Ends
By Adding Finishing
Pieces As Necessary

FINISH LEFT &
RIGHT ENDS OF
BORDER

CHAIN LINK BORDER: A WIDE BORDER WITH LOTS OF ATTENTION CENTERED ON TWO ZIGZAG LINES.

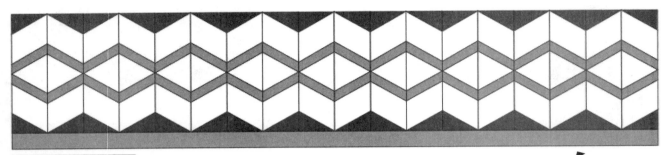

Inner Border

1. Cut for one Chain Link Strip:

1.	1 light	3½"	triangle
2.	2 dark	3¾"	triangle half

2. Sew a dark 1¼" and a light 2½" strip together lengthwise. Make two of these. Press right sides together, lining edges up carefully. Trim either end to a 60° angle. Then cut 3¼" sections from this set of strips. You will get a stripped diamond and its reverse.

3. With the pieces listed above, plus a stripped diamond and a reverse stripped diamond, assemble a Chain Link Strip as shown. Sew two Chain Link Strips together as shown to make one link. Add links to make the right length border. 12 links were used for each left and right border of the *Floral Flamenco* quilt, and 13 links top and bottom. To help fit the borders, a 1⅞" inner border was used top and bottom, and a 2" inner border left and right.

4. The border can overlap to fill the corners, with or without inner borders, as in the Floral Flamenco quilt. Or try it with corners that can be filled with: a half-square (from large 90° triangles ½" bigger than the width of the border) or a plain square the same size as the finished border width. Add an appliqué stacked repeat hexagon to each corner if desired.

Trim to 60°

#2

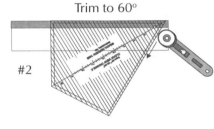

Cut Stripped Diamonds

Chain Link Strip

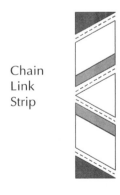

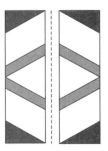

Pair Of Strips Makes One Link

84

Tipi Border: An active border with a folk-art look. It might be perfect on your quilt.

Half-Triangle

This border is made from parts of the **MOTHER OF PEARL** block. Directions:
1. Sew a light and a dark 2⅛" strip together lengthwise. Cut 3¾" triangles from this strip set. Trim ¼" off the bottom. (Stripped Triangle A)

2. Sew a 2¾" medium strip and a 2⅝" light strip together lengthwise. Cut 4⅞" triangles from this strip set. (Stripped Triangle B)

3. Cut:

1.	6	dark	1⅞"	diamond
2.	6	light	3½"	flat pyramid from
				1⅞" strip

4. Use the pieces listed above, plus Stripped Triangle A to assemble a Tipi triangle as shown. Add enough of both Tipi triangles and Stripped Triangle B to make the desired length border. Pam used 12 Tipi triangles for each left and right border of the *Mother Of Pearl* quilt, and eleven Tipi triangles top and bottom. To help fit the borders, a narrow inner border was used on all four sides.

5. Square off the ends of each border section with a stripped triangle half. *(Trim a stripped triangle to half plus seam allowance.)* The border can overlap to fill the corners, with or without inner borders, as in the Floral Flamenco quilt. Or try it with corners that can be filled with: a half-square (from large 90° triangles ½" bigger than the width of the border) or a plain square the same size as the finished border width. Add an appliqué stacked repeat hexagon to each corner if desired.

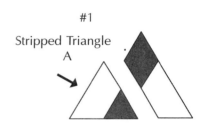

#1
Stripped Triangle
A

Tipi Triangle

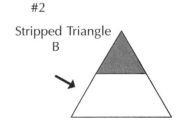

#2
Stripped Triangle
B

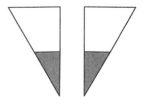

Stripped Triangle
Left and Right Half

Arizona Star Border: A new twist on a western look, this is a surprisingly easy border to piece.

Pieced Strip A

Pieced Strip B
And Reverse

This border is made from parts of the WEAVE block. Directions:

1. Sew a dark and light 2⅛" strip right sides together with a quarter inch seam down both sides. Cut triangles from the set of strips. Open and press to the dark. Add one dark 2⅛" triangle to make Pieced Strip A as shown. Make 4 of these for one border unit. Take two and add a light 1⅞" diamond to make Pieced strip B and its reverse. Sew onto a 3¼" diamond as shown.

2. Square off each border unit with two left and two right 6¾" triangle halves (cut from a 3⅞" x 6¾" rectangle). Make enough Arizona Star Border units to assemble the desired length border. Joan used twelve border units for each left and right border of *Butterflies In The Willows* quilt, and ten border units top and bottom. She added a square of fabric with an appliqué flower in each corner to complete this striking border.

Piecing
Diagram

Arizona Star
Border Unit

Cut Triangle Halves
From a 3⅞" x 6¾"
Rectangle

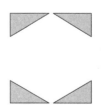

Square Off With Left And
Right 6¾" Triangle Halves

Ice Cream Border: A simple pattern inspired by the scalloped-edge look of many thirties quilts.

Directions:

1. Cut a 3¼" diamond. Trim a 1⅝" off one end to produce a gem shape. Cut a 3½" background triangle and a 2⅛" background triangle and sew into a diagonal pieced strip as shown. Make 20 of these strips for the left and right borders and 15 units for the top and bottom borders.

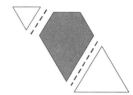

Piecing
Diagram

2. Square off each border panel with a left or right end piece assembled from a 4" left or right background triangle half, 2⅝" left or right background triangle half, and a 2⅛" triangle.

Diagonal
Pieced Strip

3. Add a 2⅝" background inner border to the quilt top on the left and right sides. Add a 2¼" background inner border to the quilt top at the top and the bottom. Sew on the left and right Ice Cream Border panels. Add 4¾" corner squares to each end of the top and bottom borders, and sew them on to the quilt top. Add a final 2" outer border to complete this graceful border for a finished quilt size with borders of 66" x 83".

Left or Right End Piece
For Ice Cream Border

End
Piece
Piecing
Diagram

Square Off Each End of the Ice Cream Border with a 4" Left or Right Triangle Half, a 2⅝" Left or Right Triangle Half, and a 2⅛" Triangle

Cut Crystal Border: Sharp and sparkly and easy to make, it can be subtle or strongly colored.

Piecing
Diagram

Directions:

1. Cut a 3¼" diamond and two 3½" background triangles. Sew into a diagonal pieced strip as shown. Make 21 of these strips for the left and right borders and 16 strips for the top and bottom borders.

2. Square off each border panel with EITHER a right 6¾" background triangle half, or right and left 4" background triangle halves as shown in the diagrams below.

3. Kathie Kryla added two narrow inner borders to the Garnet quilt top. Then she sewed on the left and right Cut Crystal Border panels. Add 6¼" corner squares to each end of the top and bottom pieced border panels, and sew them on to the quilt top. (You can either applique' stacked repeat hexes to these squares, or use 4" triangle halves to square the hexes up.) Add a final narrow outer border to complete this graceful look.

Diagonal
Pieced Strip

Left or Right End Pieces
For Cut Crystal Border

Square Off Each End of the Cut Crystal Border with a 6¾"
Right Triangle Half OR with 4" Left & Right Triangle Halves

TRIANGLES BORDER: THE SIMPLEST BORDER OF ALL. MAKE IT LARGE OR SMALL (OR BOTH). ADJUSTS EASILY.

Directions:

1. Sew and cut matching triangles the size desired (usually 3½" or 2⅛"). Sew into a pieced strip as shown above. When you press the strip, be careful not to stretch it lengthwise. (This border easily stretches a little to fit your quilt top.)

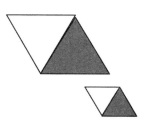

Sandwich-pieced
Matching Triangles

2. Square off each border panel with a right or left background triangle half that is cut ½" bigger than the size of the matching triangle. You may wish to fill the corner with a square cut the same size as the matching triangle.

Sew Into Pieced Strip

3. Linda DeGaeta used a triangles border on Emmanuel Starlight. A good way to use leftover stripped triangles is to sew them into a triangles border. Simple and effective.

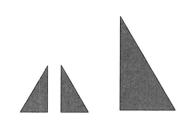

Left or Right End Pieces
For Triangles Border

Square Off Each End of any Triangles Border with a Left or Right Triangle Half Cut ½" Larger than the Sandwich-pieced Triangle

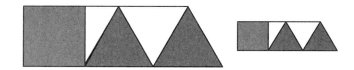

SCALLOP BORDER: A BIT OF FUN, LIKE THE FLAGS AND FLOUNCES OF A CIRCUS OR PARADE.

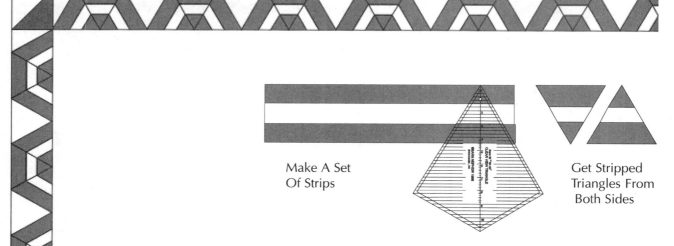

Make A Set Of Strips

Get Stripped Triangles From Both Sides

Directions:

1. Sew a set of three strips together lengthwise to make 3½" stripped triangles. The two outside strips should be the same fabric, so you can use the triangles from both sides of the set of strips. You may want to draw the triangle and try drawing in different strip widths. The two outside strips should be the same width. (Try three 1½" strips.)

2. Cut 3½" triangles from the set of strips. Sew three stripped triangles together as shown to make one scallop. You will need background 3½" triangles to go between the scallops. Because the scallops are large, either add an inner border to the quilt top to help it fit the pieced border panels, or make a size adjustment with a fancy center to each border panel.

3. Square off each border panel with right and left 4" background triangle halves. Sew the left and right border panels to the quilt top. Add 3¼" squares on the left and right ends of the top and bottom pieced border panels. Or try half-squares (cut 3⅝" squares in half diagonally) of two fabrics to make a different kind of corner.

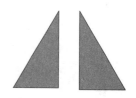

Piecing Diagram

Left and Right Triangle Half

Add 3¼" Squares Or Half-Squares For Corners

String Of Pearls Border: A great way to add more stacked repeat Hexagons to your quilt.

Directions:

1. If you have extra fabric, you can cut and sew more stacked hexagons from 3½" triangles to use as a border. After you have the stacked hexes, cut 3½" background triangles. Sew two background triangles on two opposite sides to make diamond-shaped units.

2. Sew units together in a row to make a border panel. Square off the ends of each panel with left and right 4" triangle halves. Add 6" wide fabric as necessary to lengthen the border panel.

3. Sew the left and right border panels to the quilt top. Add 6" corner squares on the left and right ends of the top and bottom pieced border panels. Or try half-squares (cut 6⅜" squares in half diagonally) of two fabrics to make a different kind of corner.

4. These stacked repeat hexagons could actually be made out of any sized triangle. If you use a different size, then the background triangle should be the same size as the triangle used in the hexagons.. And the triangle half should be cut from a triangle ½" bigger than the triangle you are working with.

Make More Stacked
Repeat Hexagons

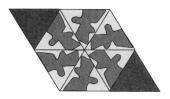

Add Background
Triangles

Left and Right
Triangle Half

Add 6" Squares or Half-
Squares For Corners

Square Off Ends With
3¾"Triangle Halves

Peekaboo Border: Half-hexes are an echo of shape and color like flower petals all around.

Directions:

1. If you have extra fabric, you can cut and sew more stacked half-hexagons from 3½" triangles to use as a border. After you have the stacked half-hexes, cut 3½" background triangles. Sew a background triangle on one end of each half-hex to make elongated diamond-shaped units.

2. Sew units together in a row to make a border panel. Square off the ends of each panel with left and right 4" triangle halves.

3. Sew the left and right border panels to the quilt top. Add 3¼" corner squares on the left and right ends of the top and bottom pieced border panels. Or try half-squares (cut 3⅞" squares in half diagonally) of two fabrics to make a different kind of corner.

4. These repeat half-hexagons could actually be made out of any sized triangle. If you use a different size, then the background triangle should be the same size as the triangle used in the half-hex. And the triangle half should be cut from a triangle ½" bigger than the triangle you are working with.

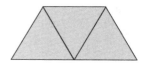

Make Stacked Repeat
Half-Hexagons

Add Background
Triangle

Left and Right
Triangle Half

Square Off Ends With
4"Triangle Halves

Add 3¼" Squares or Half-
Squares For Corners

WHAT IF? BIG BORDERS ON SMALL QUILTS

THESE DRAWINGS MAY INSPIRE YOU TO TRY DIFFERENT COMBINATIONS OF BLOCKS & BORDERS

Amber Wallhanging With Ice
Cream Border (above)

Garnet Runner With
Diamond Lace Border (right)

Dark Eyes 5-block Wallhanging
With Scallop Border (below)

Comet 3-block Wallhanging With
Two Triangle Borders (above)

Native 2-row Wallhanging With Cut
Crystal Border (above)

*Perhaps the border will repeat a unit
in the quilt, or just pick up and echo
a general movement of the design.
The Scallop Border echos the curves
in the Dark Eyes Wallhanging.*

VISUAL INDEX - 2-ROW QUILT LAYOUTS

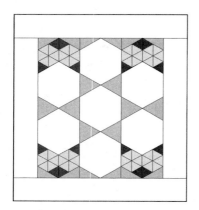

Sara's Simple Layout pg. 95

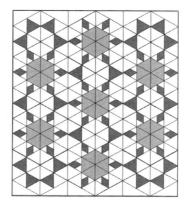

Setting Triangles Layout pg. 96

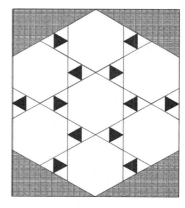

Plain Corners pg. 96

Half-Block Corners pg. 97

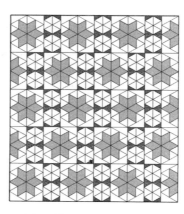

Hex Spacers pg. 98

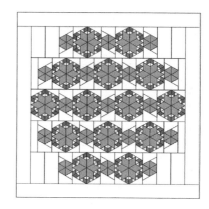

Plain Spacers pg. 98

Alternate Blocks pg. 96

Janet's Amber Layout pg. 96

Combination Layout (below) pg. 99
One 3-Row block surrounded by six
2-Row blocks makes a striking
arrangement. Try your artistry!

Ideas are shown here on paper that haven't all been sewn into quilts.
You have a chance to be the first, if you like a particular layout. The
pattern testers in this book came up with ideas at different times
independently of each other. For example, the half-block corner was
seen first in Bonnie Chamber's quilt, but others used it with 3-row
blocks as their own idea. Guess great minds think alike!

Sara's Simple Layout

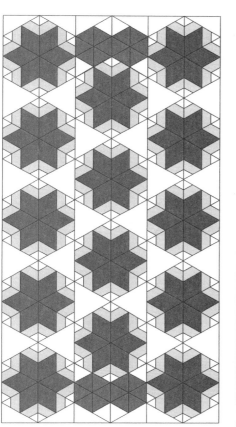

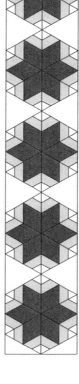

Piecing Diagram (above)

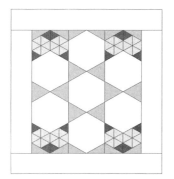
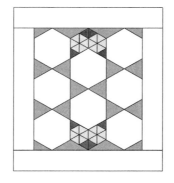

The number of blocks needed for a quilt depends on how you decide to arrange them. The two little baby quilts shown above have seven OR eight blocks included, depending on the layout.

3½" triangle
Sara's Simple Layout
Without Borders: 55½" x 64¼"

POSSIBLE 6¼"
SETTING TRIANGLES

The BORDER BLOCK is shown in Sara's Simple Layout (diagram at left). This arrangement can be made any size. **SHOWN - 5 blocks High and 5 Blocks wide. Quilt Without Borders - 55½" x 64¼"** You will need 23 blocks and eight stacked repeat hexagons. Choices are possible in setting triangles, see above right, and any 2-Row block will fit into this layout. Some examples are shown below, but see pg. 14 for many more choices.

To Square Off the Top & Bottom of Each Row, Cut Triangle Halves From Two 6¾" x 3¢" Rectangles, One Right Side Up, and One Wrong Side Up

Sara's Simple Layout Variations
Plain Corners and Pieced Setting Triangles Add Even More Possibilities

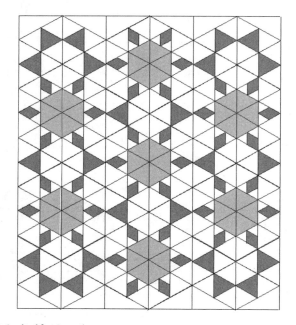

Plain half-triangle corners concentrate attention on the hexagon medallion formed by seven 2-Row blocks (upper right). And pieced setting triangles of any kind form subsidiary designs, both between the blocks and when used to create a special corner section (above).

Janet's Amber Layout

JANET'S AMBER LAYOUT (bottom left, *see quilt in color on pg. 50*) puts blocks edge to edge for a different look entirely. This layout is also possible using 3-Row blocks. What if you combine two different blocks for new subsidiary patterns? Add pieced setting triangles and the possibilities are endless. Shown below is a wallhanging illustrating the combination of SIMPLE STAR and TINY STAR.

HALF-BLOCK CORNER LAYOUT

3½" triangle
7-Block Quilt With Half-Block Corners
Without Borders: 33½" x 42"

This arrangement can be made in many sizes. But sometimes creative piecing solutions will be required. See the Piecing Diagram for an 11-Block Quilt below right. Yet, using half-blocks creates a beautiful solution for corners, fill-in pieces, even borders. And it allows the quilter to make and use many more stacked repeat hexagons. *See Kathy Kryla's* **Morning** *quilt on pg. 69.*

Piecing Diagram of 1-Block Quilt With Half-Block Corners

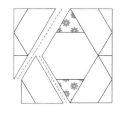 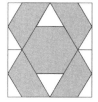

Note from the author: Bonnie Chambers produced the first version of the half-block corner layout that I saw. But other pattern testers had done the same thing, which I didn't see until they turned their quilts in. Linda Degaeta and Kathy Kryla both found good uses for half-block layouts. I used the layout idea in a very large 2-Row block quilt from the TATTLER block. (Inside Front cover) That queen-sized bed quilt uses 45 complete blocks and eight partial blocks. Some coping strips were part of the plan to put the whole quilt together, and they provide a little float space top and bottom.

Piecing Diagram of an 11-Block Quilt With Half-Block Corners & Borders

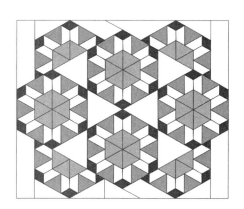

The DAISY block (left) in a 4-Block Wall Hanging With Half-Block Corners

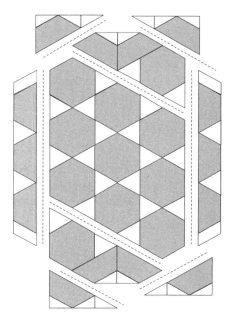

SPACERS MAKE GREAT LAYOUTS

OFFSET STAR QUILT

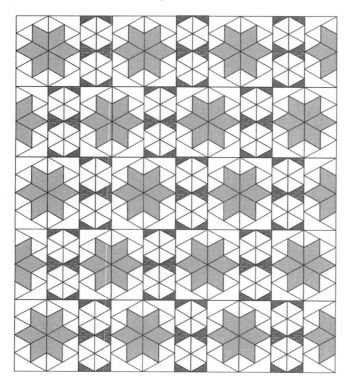

3½" triangle
Offset Star Quilt
Without Borders: 55½" x 64¼"

A plain piece of fabric the width of half a block and the height of a block is useful in many quilt layouts. Use it to add space anywhere in a row of blocks. Make a spacer with a stacked repeat (or two) in it to scatter twirls, flowers, stars, etc., wherever you want in your quilt. Here are a couple of layouts for you to try.

Assembly Directions For Offset Star Quilt:
Make 30 2-Row blocks and five left or right half-blocks. Square off these units with left and right 6¾" background triangle halves. Make spacers from two 3½" triangle stacked repeat hexagons, two 3½" background triangles, and two each left and right 4" triangle halves. Make 15 spacers altogether. Assemble as shown.

3½" triangle
Circle Of Stars
Without Borders: 33½" x 29"

Assembly Directions For Circle Of Stars:
Make 14 two-row blocks. Square off these blocks with left and right 6¾" background triangle halves. Make spacers from: one 3½" triangle stacked repeat hexagon, two 3½" background triangles, and two each 4¾" x 6¼" rectangles trimmed to a 60° angle as shown below. Make 17 pieced spacers altogether. Cut eight 6" x 13¼" background fabric spacers. Cut four 3¼" x 13¾" background fabric spacers. Assemble according to the diagram.

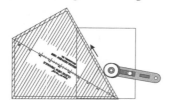

CIRCLE OF STARS

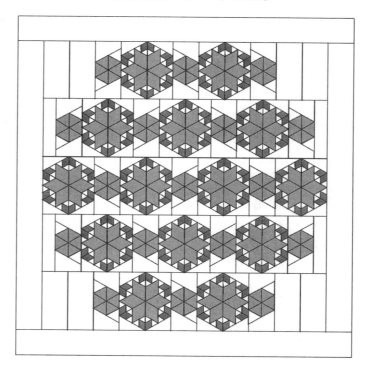

3½" triangle
Combination Quilt
Without Borders: 33½" x 29"

To produce a gorgeous wallhanging or throw quilt, use your choice of any 3-Row block design and six coordinating 2-Row blocks put together in this stunning quilt layout. This example shows DARK EYES as the 3-Row block and FROST as the six 2-Row blocks. Linda DeGaeta used MORNING LIGHT and NATIVE in her quilts (pg. 54). Without corners and borders, the hexagon-shaped wallhanging measures 39" x 49½". Square off the hexagon with left and right triangle halves cut from a 13" x 22" rectangle. (Place two rectangles right or wrong sides together and cut corner-to-corner.)

13" x 22" Rectangle Bisected

Pieced Triangle and Pieced Strip

Assembly Directions:
Make a three-row block for the center and six two-row blocks to surround it. Six setting triangles with stacked repeats make the star points. To put it all together, six pieced triangles and six pieced strips are added to make side sections #1, #2, and #3. Sew them onto the center triangle in order. Add corners and borders to complete the quilt.

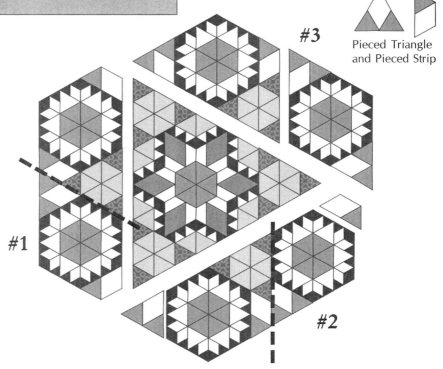

VISUAL INDEX - 3-ROW QUILT LAYOUTS

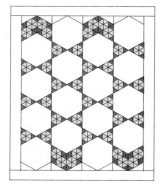

16-Block Quilt, pg. 103

10-Block Quilt, pg. 104

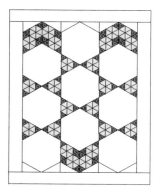

9-Block Quilt, pg. 105

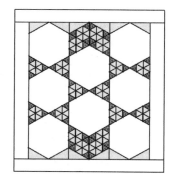

8-Block Quilt, pg. 106

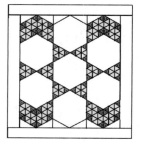

7-Block Quilt, pg. 107

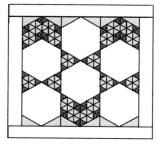

6-Block Quilt, pg. 106

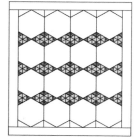

Even 16-Block Quilt, pg. 110

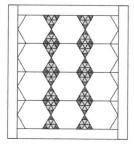

Even 12-Block Quilt, pg. 110

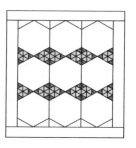

Even 9-Block Quilt, pg. 110

Half-Block Corners, pg. 107

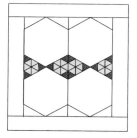

4-Block Quilt, pg. 108

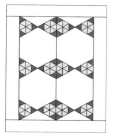

4-Block Quilt, pg. 110

4-Block Quilt, pg. 108

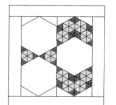

3-Block Quilt, pg. 102

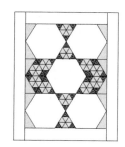

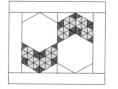

2-Block Quilt, pg. 109

Shown Right:
The Fancy 7-Block Quilt is a difficult layout. Put it on a wall or floor and be sure you have it right before you start sewing. The Piecing Diagram is shown on pg. 111.

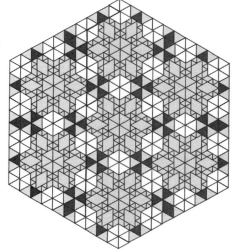

The 10-Block Quilt, the 7-Block Quilt, and the 4-Block Quilt have Half-block, Triangle Half and Star corners as extra layout possibilities. Not shown on this page: 1-Block Quilt, pg. 109; Table Runner #1, pg. 102; Table Runner #2, pg. 105.

PUTTING IT ALL TOGETHER - 3-ROW BLOCK QUILTS

When you have made as many 3-row blocks as you wish, or as many as you can get from your fabric, you can start to think about setting triangles and quilt layouts. The kind of setting triangle you choose will make a BIG difference in the final appearance of your quilt. Also, depending on the quilt layout you choose in the following pages, you will need to make more or less setting triangles. So flip through these pages and see what appeals to you before you sew too many of the setting triangles.

SETTING TRIANGLES

To construct a Serendipity Setting Triangle, sew six layered pattern repeat (center*) triangles into two sets of three, pin to match centers and sew across the middle. Sew three background fabric 3½" triangles onto three separate sides of the resulting pieced hexagon.

The basic setting triangle is made from:

6	center*	3½"	triangles
3	accent	3½"	triangles

Pieced Hexagon

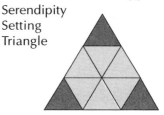
Serendipity Setting Triangle

SUBSTITUTIONS & VARIATIONS

In this second book, quiltmakers seemed more confident, more willing to try new things. So they created new setting triangle variations, new layouts, and new borders. Just having fun, I guess! To add another design element to the quilt, or if you run out of pattern repeats, try substituting these hexagons in the setting triangles.

1. A hexagon made from 3½" triangles of two different fabrics sewed alternately.

Six 3½" Triangles

2. A hexagon cut from a 6" strip. (Cut a 6" diamond, then cut a 3" trangle from each end.) Find a pretty motif and center the hexagon on this.

6" Hexagon

3. A little star made from 1⅞" diamonds and 2⅛" triangles. Sew two triangles to a diamond. Press to the triangles. Make six of these pieced triangles. Sew three and three. Press out from the center. Pinch and pin the center. Sew across the middle.

1⅞" Diamonds & 2⅛" Triangles

4. A little star made from 2⅛" triangles. Assemble six wedges. Sew three and three, pressing out. Pinch, pin, and sew as in #3.

2⅛" Triangles

Whatever you put in place of the stacked repeat 6" hexagon, you should usually sew three 3½" triangles (light, medium, or dark fabric as you choose) on three seperate sides of the hex to make a Serendipity Setting Triangle. Unless you are using a pieced or solid 9" triangle.

5. A hexagon cut from a 4" strip. Add three flat pyramids cut from a 1½"strip at 2½". Then add three flat pyramids cut from a 1½" strip at 4½" on the Super 60°.

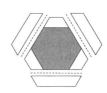

6. A star with diamond points. Make six pieced diamond units from sets of strips as in MORNING STAR, pg. 41. Be sure the color intended to form the center star is at the points of the diamonds. Sew units three and three to make a star. Trim away alternate points as shown. Courtesy of Linda De Gaeta.

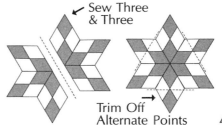
Sew Three & Three
Trim Off Alternate Points

Pieced Star Setting Triangle
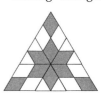

Or even more variety: substitute a solid 9" triangle or three diamonds and three triangles to make a different setting triangle.

Pieced 9" Triangle

Plain 9" Triangle

FINISH THE QUILT TOP

Sew blocks and setting triangles into vertical rows as shown in the quilt diagram you choose. Different quilt layouts require different numbers of blocks and setting triangles. Rows (often) alternately begin with a block at the top and four setting triangles to finish the bottom, or the other way around. Square off both ends of each row with triangle halves cut from a 5½" x 9½" rectangle.

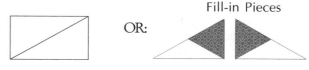

OR:

Fill-in Pieces

Cut Triangle Halves From a 5½" x 9½" Rectangle

4⅞" triangle plus 2⅞" diamond half

OR: Square off both ends of each row with a Fill-In Piece constructed from a 4⅞" triangle plus a 2⅞" diamond half . Sew the rows together as shown in the quilt diagram. Complete with borders as desired.

3½" triangle	3-Block Table Runner #1	**Without Borders: 17" x 77"**

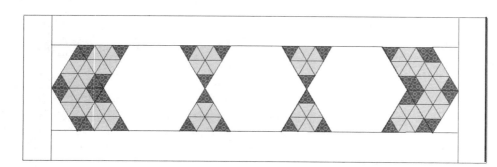

This 3-Block Table Runner is easy to put together as a fancy touch for a special dinner. You may use leftover blocks to make this easy project. Make a shorter table runner by leaving off the setting triangles at each end (see pg. 105).

3½" triangle
3-Block Quilt
Without Borders: 33½" x 38¾"

10 Setting Triangles:
(30 background 3½" triangles)
7" accent fabric for setting triangles
5½" fabric for fill-in pieces

The 3-Block Quilt is assembled in two vertical rows, with one row having two blocks and two setting triangles, and the second row having one block and eight setting triangles. With borders, it is exactly baby quilt size. Extra blocks can make this great little quilt.

Piecing Diagram

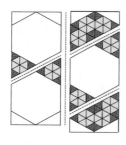

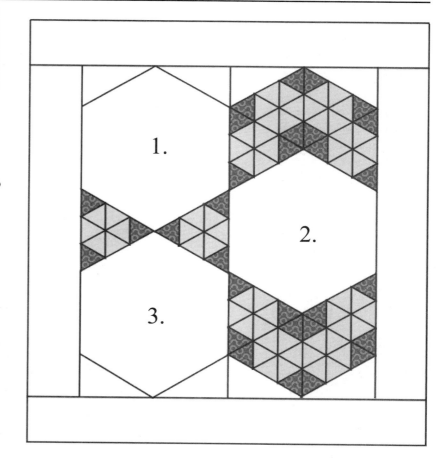

1.

2.

3.

All fabrics 42" wide prewashed.

Fabric Requirements: these are suggestions and estimates.

First - Up to four high contrast large print fabrics – each with six repeats

40 Setting Triangles: (120 background 3½" triangles)

1 yd. fabric for 3½" background triangles

½ yd. fabric for fill-in pieces at top and bottom

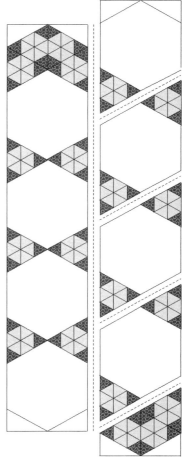

3½" triangle		
16-Block Quilt		
Without Borders: 76½" x 95"		

IF stacked repeat shape in block is:

3½" triangle	Minimum Needed	2 yd. fabric
3¼" diamond		2¼ yd.
4⅞" triangle		2½ yd.
4⅝" diamond		3¼ yd.
6¼" triangle		3½ yd.

Piecing Diagram

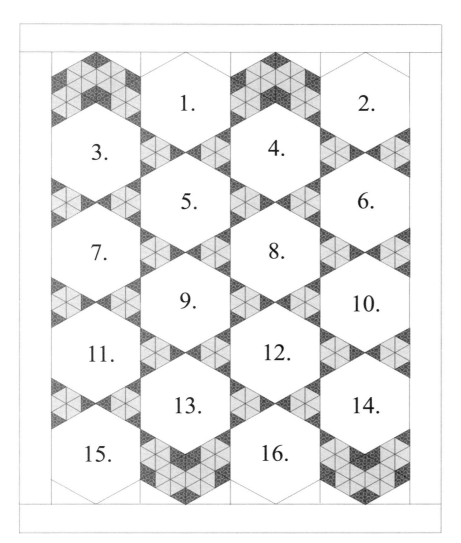

Piece the quilt in vertical rows of four blocks each. Each block begins with a block and ends with four setting triangles as shown. The second and fourth row are turned upside down. Lay out the blocks and setting triangles on a floor or wall for the best arrangement before beginning to sew the blocks into rows. Then sew the rows together to make the quilt top. Add borders as desired.

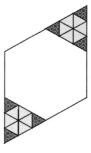

Basic Units

10-Block Quilt

Without Borders: 50" x 77"

All fabrics 42" wide prewashed.
Fabric Requirements:
These are suggestions and estimates.
30 Setting Triangles:
(90 background 3½" triangles)
1 yd. fabric for setting triangles
⅓" yd. fabric for fill-in pieces

No piecing diagram is given. The quilt is pieced in three rows. The center row consists of four blocks and six setting triangles. The two ouside rows each have three blocks and 12 setting triangles. Or, make three rows as in the variation below right, squaring off the elongated hexagon with left and right triangle halves cut from a 16" x 27½" rectangle. (Place two rectangles right or wrong sides together and cut corner-to-corner.) If you use the triangle half corners, or the star corners, fabric requirements will be different.

16" x 27½" Rectangle Bisected

See pg. 107 for more instructions on how to put together the Star Corner, including a piecing diagram. Choices of fabric, judging color, pattern, texture and value add to or subtract from the effectiveness of any design or layout. But it's fun to learn!

With Star Corners

With Triangle Half Corners

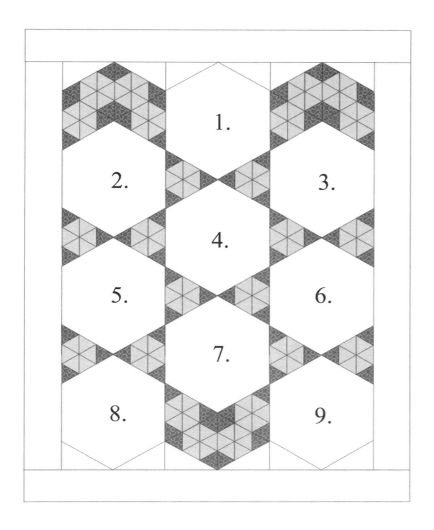

All fabrics 42" wide prewashed.
Fabric Requirements: these are suggestions and estimates.
One high contrast large print fabric – six repeats
24 Setting Triangles: (72 background 3½" triangles)
½ yd. fabric background triangles
⅓ yd. fabric for fill-in pieces at top and bottom

Piecing Diagram

The 9-Block Quilt is assembled in three identical vertical rows, with the center row turned upside down. With borders, it makes a twin-sized quilt. It's big enough to have fun with, giving lots of variety in the block designs and setting triangles, while small enough not to become a chore. As a diagram, it shows enough blocks to demonstrate secondary designs created in a quilt layout, and so the author used it on each page of the block designs.

3½" triangle   3-Block Table Runner #2   Without Borders: 17" x 57½"

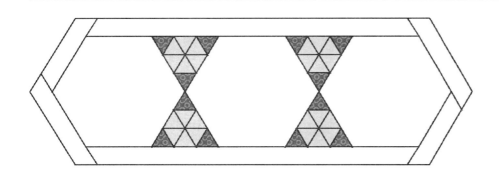

This smaller Table Runner is quick to make, with only the three blocks and four setting triangles in all. A narrow outside border finishes it off as an elongated hexagon. Or, square it off, like the table runner on pg. 102.

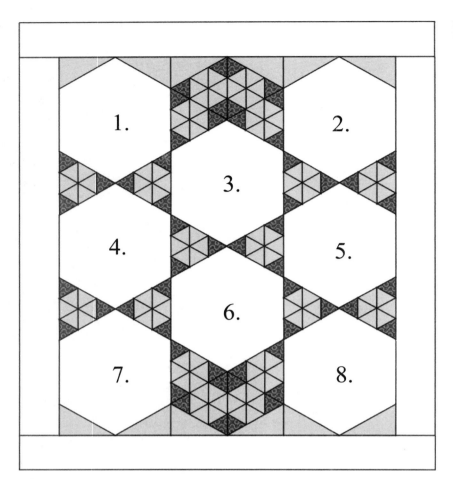

The 8-Block Quilt is assembled in three vertical rows, with three blocks and four setting triangles in the outside rows, and two blocks and 10 setting triangles in the center row. Fill-in pieces are added to each row as shown, before the rows are sewn together. With borders, it makes a twin sized quilt. Another very populay layout.

All fabrics 42" wide prewashed.
Fabric Requirements:
suggestions and estimates
18 Setting Triangles:
(54 background 3½" triangles)
½ yd. fabric for setting triangles
⅓ yd. fabric for fill-in pieces

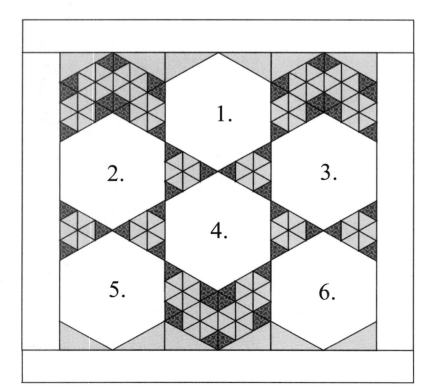

3½" triangle
6-Block Quilt
Without Borders: 50" x 48½"

The 6-Block Quilt is assembled in three vertical rows, with two blocks and six setting triangles in each row. The center row is assembled upside down. Fill-in pieces are added to each row as shown, before the rows are sewn together. With borders, it makes a wall hanging or throw.

All fabrics 42" wide prewashed.
Fabric Requirements:
suggestions and estimates
18 Setting Triangles:
(54 background 3½" triangles)
½ yd. fabric for setting triangles
⅓ yd. fabric for fill-in pieces

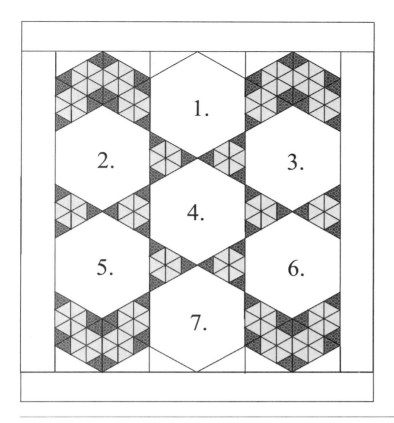

Piecing Diagram

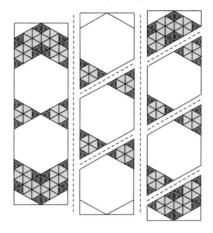

All fabrics 42" wide prewashed.
Fabric Requirements:
suggestions and estimates
24 Setting Triangles:
(72 background 3½" triangles)
¾ yd. fabric for setting triangles
⅓ yd. fabric for fill-in pieces

The half-block layout shown below actually uses nine blocks altogether, and has an especially rich and textured look. Square off the half-blocks top and bottom with 9½" triangle halves as on star corners on left. Cut 4⅝" strips and trim to a 60° angle for other spacing strips.

You can float a star in the corners of your 10-Block, 7-Block or 4-Block quilt. The large background triangles are 6¼" and the other pieces needed are fill-in pieces: 3¼" diamonds, 3½" triangles, a 3¼" strip trimmed to a 60° angle, and a diamond half cut from a 2⅞" strip.

Star Corners

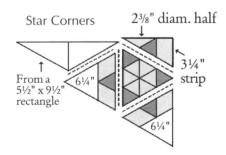

2⅜" diam. half

From a 5½" x 9½" rectangle

6¼"

3¼" strip

6¼"

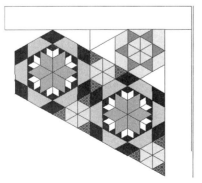

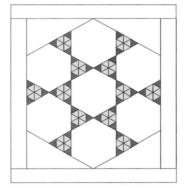

Triangle Half Corners

An alternate version of the 7-Block quilt squares off the hexagon with left and right triangle halves from a 16" x 27½" rectangle. (See pg. 103. Or cut a larger than 26" triangle, cut it in half down the center, and trim to square up after the triangle halves are sewn on.) The 4-Block quilt can also use these large triangle halves for less work and a faster finish. Or put stars in the corners of your quilt for a different look.

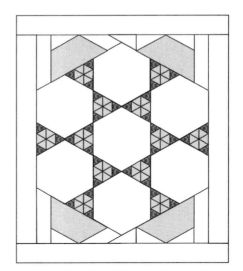

107

3½" triangle
5-Block Quilt
Without Borders: 33½" x 50"

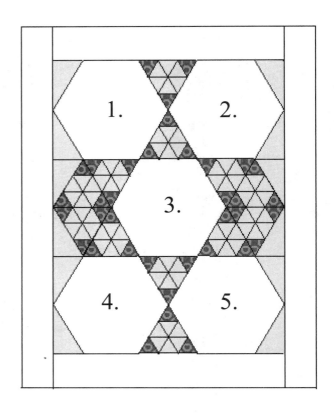

The 5-Block Quilt is assembled in three horizontal rows, with two blocks and two setting triangles in the top and bottom row, and one block and eight setting triangles in the center row. Fill-in pieces are added to each row as shown, before the rows are sewn together. With borders, it makes a wallhanging or child's quilt.

All fabrics 42" wide prewashed.
Fabric Requirements: suggestions and estimates
12 Setting Triangles: (36 background 3½" triangles)
⅓ yd. background fabric for setting triangles
5½" fabric for fill-in pieces

3½" triangle
4-Block Quilt
Without Borders: 50" x 33½"

10 Setting Triangles:
(30 background 3½" triangles)
7" fabric for setting triangles
5½" fabric for fill-in pieces

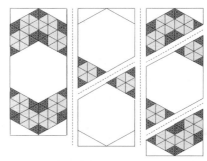

Piecing Diagram

The 4-Block Quilt is assembled in three vertical rows, with the center row having two blocks and two setting triangles, and the two end rows having one block and eight setting triangles each as shown. With borders, it is a good size wallhanging. A fast variation uses only six setting triangles, squaring off the resulting diamond shape with left and right triangle halves cut from 16" x 27½" rectangles. (See pg. 104.)

With Triangle Half Corners

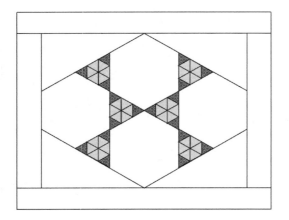

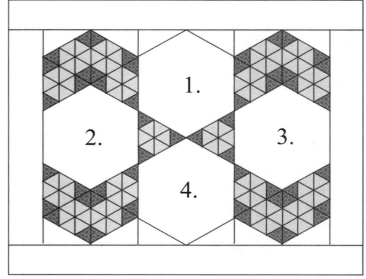

108

3½" triangle
2-Block Quilt
Without Borders: 33½" x 29"

All fabrics 42" wide prewashed.
Fabric Requirements: suggestions and estimates
8 Setting Triangles: (24 background 3½" triangles)
7" strip of fabric for setting triangles
5½" fabric for fill-in pieces

The 2-Block Quilt is assembled in two identical vertical rows, with one row turned upside down. With borders, it makes a small wallhanging. Leftover blocks and setting triangles make a gift quilt, or a small quilt can become an experiment in pattern and color.

Piecing Diagram

 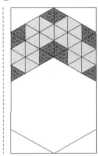

3½" triangle
1-Block Quilt
Without Borders: 25¼" x 33½"

Piecing Diagrams

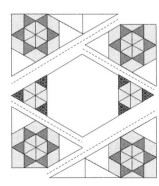

The 1-Block Quilt is assembled with a diamond in the center and four identical sets of three setting triangles each, with fill-in pieces added as shown. With borders, it makes a small wallhanging. One leftover block with setting triangles or their substitutes, can be an art project or a great gift. Try substituting Star Corners for the twelve setting triangles.

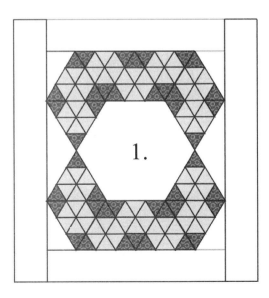

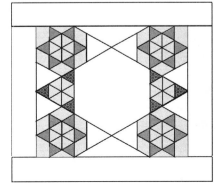

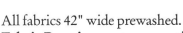

All fabrics 42" wide prewashed.
Fabric Requirements: suggestions and estimates
14 Setting Triangles: (42 background 3½" triangles)
⅓ yd. fabric for setting triangles
5½" fabric for fill-in pieces

EDGE TO EDGE LAYOUTS

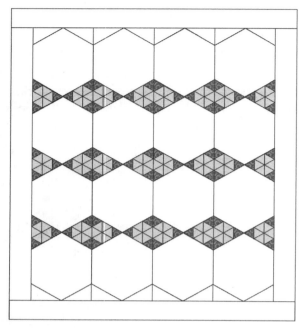

16-Block Quilt
Quilt Without Borders: 66½" x 73¾"

12-Block Quilt
Quilt Without Borders: 54¾" x 66½"

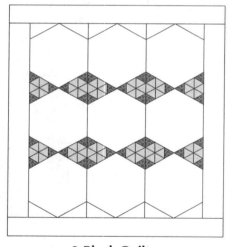

9-Block Quilt
Quilt Without Borders: 50" x 54¾"

4-Block Quilt
Quilt Without Borders: 33½" x 48¼"

4-Block Quilt Alternate
Quilt Without Borders: 33½" x 35½"

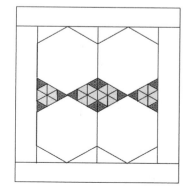

Placing blocks lined up with each other, edge to edge, instead of offsetting them with setting triangles opens up more design possibilities. Consider these layouts after you have finished enough blocks to imagine how your quilt is going to look. Janet Goad used this layout with a 2-Row block. (See **Asian Jewels** quilt on pg. 60 and "Janet's Amber Layout" on pg. 96.) Of course, with 2-Row blocks the stacked repeat hexagon setting triangles as shown are too big to use. But they fit with 3-Row blocks. Will these layouts look good with 3-Row blocks? What about using a different setting triangle between the blocks? Sometimes colored pencils and graph paper will help make the possibilities clearer.

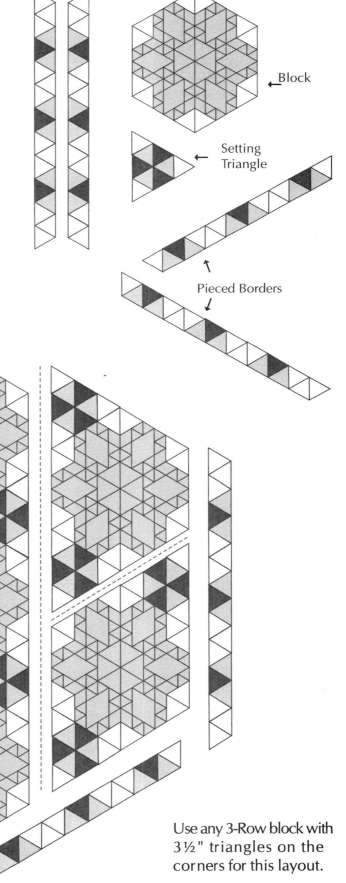

3½" triangle
Fancy 7-Block Quilt
Without Borders: 33½" x 29"

To see an example of this layout, turn to Joan Dawson's **Butterflies In The Willows** on pg. 51. Arrange according to the diagram: Each **white** triangle is part of a stacked repeat hexagon, but also may be part of the star block. **Dark** triangles complete star points. **Gray** shapes can complete diamond shapes between stars, or they are part of the star. This is a complicated layout that takes a lot of concentration. You may wish to add pieced borders as shown at right to complete all the stacked repeat hexagons around the edges of the blocks. Sew into a 7-block layout as shown.

←Block

Setting
Triangle

Pieced Borders

Four Corner
Triangle Halves are
from 17" x 28¾" rectangles

Use any 3-Row block with
3½" triangles on the
corners for this layout.

OTHER PRODUCTS FROM CLEARVIEW TRIANGLE

60° Triangle Books and Tools

SQ-29	$27.95	Book - Serendipity Quilts
B-25	19.95	Book - Big Book Of Building Block Quilts
B-21	14.95	Book - Sensational 6-Pointed Star Quilts
SR-20	16.95	Super 60 (Combination Triangle Tool)
DG-27	6.75	Diamond Guide (Super 60 Add-On)
MP-3	13.75	8" Mini-Pro
CT-1	9.95	6" triangle
CT-2	18.00	12" triangle
GP-12	5.95	2-sided Graph Paper-Pad of 30 sheets
M-15	13.75	Metric Triangle
M-23	16.95	Metric Super 60

Bargain Corner

QA-28	$9.00	Book - Quilted Adventures
ZO 18	15.00	Book - Patchwork Zoo
EA –7	5.00	Book - Easy & Elegant Quilts
MA-14	5.00	Book - Mock Appliqué
HH-17	4.00	Book - Happy Halloween
TX-23	4.00	Book - Special Times
TC-24	4.00	Book - Town & Country
MC-16	4.00	Book - Merry Christmas
NL-19	3.00	Book - New Labels
PR-22	3.00	Pattern - Pigma® Pen Roll-Up

Order From:
CLEARVIEW TRIANGLE
8311 - 180th St S. E.
Snohomish, WA 98296
Tel: 1-360-668-4151
Fax: 1-360-668-6338
Orders: 1-888-901-4151
E-mail: sara@clearviewtriangle.com
Website: www.clearviewtriangle.com

Special Thanks To These Manufacturers:
Andover Fabrics/Makower uk
Blank Textiles, Inc.
Free Spirit Fabric
P&B Textiles
Kelsul, Inc. Quilter's "Dream" Cotton™ Batting

To learn more about stacked pattern repeats,
read Bethany Reynolds' books, "Magic Stack 'N
Whack Quilts®", "Stack 'N Whackier," and "Magic
Quilts-By The Slice ."

Contact Bethany Reynolds:
B&R Design, Inc.
P.O. Box 1374
Ellsworth, ME 04605
Website: http://www.quilt.com/BReynolds

Shipping Charges:

Order Amount	Shipping
0.00 - 5.99	$1.99
6.00 - 10.99	2.99
11.00 - 20.99	3.99
21.00 - 30.99	4.99
31.00 - 40.99	5.99
41.00 - 65.99	6.99
66.00 - 100.99	7.99
101.00 +	9.00

International customers may have
additional shipping costs.
Wash. residents add 8.9% sales tax.
Tools usually shipped UPS,
Books U.S. Mail.
We take Visa and Mastercard.

Fractal Flowers (facing page back), 86" x 99".
The LOTUS block was so much fun to make out
of decorator fabric that the author didn't stop
until the quilt was big enough to lay across her
queen-sized bed. A printed floral stripe border,
carefully cut, makes a nice finish for the edge.
Machine quilted by Judy Irish.

Daisy Splash (facing page right), 67½" x 71".
Fun fabrics combine with the RUFFLES block in
an unusual color scheme, daisies and raindrops,
plaids and polka dots, hot pink and olive green. A
light-hearted quilt to take on a picnic. Pieced by
Virginia Anderson.

Cranes In My Garden (facing page left),
69" x 77". Gorgeous details in the stacked repeat
hexagons are held in check by strong multiple
borders that emphasize the hexagon shape. Some
of the setting triangles are centered on plain
hexagons that give samples of the fabric choice
and show the cranes. Pieced and machine quilted
by Janice Hairston.